REVELATION OF LIFE ETERNAL

NICHOLAS ARSENIEV

REVELATION OF LIFE ETERNAL

An Introduction to the Christian Message

ST. VLADIMIR'S SEMINARY PRESS
CRESTWOOD, NEW YORK
1982

Library of Congress Cataloging in Publication Data

Arsen'ev, Nikolai Sergeevich, 1888-
  Revelation of life eternal.

  Includes bibliographical references.
  1. Religion—Addresses, essays, lectures.
2. Christianity—Essence, genius, nature—
Addresses, essays, lectures. I. Title.
BL50.A8 1982   201   82-5455
ISBN 0-913836-00-1   AACR2

First published 1963

PRINTED IN THE UNITED STATES OF AMERICA
BY
ATHENS PRINTING COMPANY
NEW YORK, NY

Contents

Introduction: The Claim of Religion 7

PART I

1 Principles of Religious Cognition 11

2 Transcendence and Immanence of God 27

3 Some Problems of the History of Religions.... 39

4 Plato's Religious Message 67

5 The Mystical Encounter 75

6 The Characteristic Features of
   the Christian Message 83

PART II

7 Suffering 91

8 The Meaning and Goal of History 99

9 Resurrection and Transfiguration 107

10 The Atonement 125

11 The Humility of God 133

12 The Law of Love 141

Contents

PART I

Introduction:
The Claim of Religion

Why is religion necessary? What is the true sense of religion? Why ought we to believe in God?

One might answer to this as follows: religion plays a role of utmost importance in the life of mankind. There is no normal human life without some kind of religion. With this statement many will be quite ready to agree. In fact is there not a craving in our heart for something Final and Absolute? And in religion this craving finds its satisfaction. Is not and has not faith in God been a refuge and comfort in tribulations and sorrow? Has not religion inspired—and does it not continue to inspire—man with heroic and selfless actions, with a power of self-dedication and sacrifice, with a creative force, with a vision of beauty subjugating and entrancing the heart? Has not some kind or other of religion been the inspiring dynamic center of human culture and achievements in older times, and to a great extent now? Has it not inspired such masterpieces of the human genius as the religious art of the Middle Ages, the French and Italian cathedrals, the paintings of the old Italian, Flemish, German masters, the Old-Russian ikon, the temples of Greece and Egypt? Has it not often inspired—in modern times also—the struggle for justice, the loving and courageous service of man to man? Do we not simply *need* religion, even in our everyday life, as the ultimate basis of our whole outlook that gives sense to life in its whole texture? All this may be easily granted, for all this is true, but from the *religious* point of view (not from the point of view of practical utilization) it does not prove the case for religion. All this is true, but insufficient. For from the religious

7

point of view there is *only one decisive claim* to be raised. The
one decisive claim which religion makes is that of *Truth*: of
being *witness to Truth*. All other points of view simply result
from this one. The civilization and culture and creative inspiration and the comforting sense of a moral support and a
happier outlook in life and death are all *rejectable* if they
are founded on Untruth. More than that: there is no real
creative impulse, no real comfort, no real inspiration except
in a Supreme Truth, in a *Divine Reality*, not just in an idea
of God. Religion is witness to *Divine Reality*, this makes it
creative—yea, *the* creative, inspiring, comforting, reshaping
and transfiguring force in our lives and in the life of mankind. Religion is witness to *Truth*. For we cannot be saved
by beautiful and touching illusions: we have to reject the
most beautiful and touching illusions, we can be saved only
by the Truth. In the *Living Reality* of God is our root and
harbor and supreme goal and the source of our strength and
the ultimate sense of life and of the life of the universe.

Of course, Truth can be distorted—and that is the case in
many religions, as we shall see in the chapter dedicated to
problems of the history of religions. There is often the inrush
of the powers of Evil into the field of religious life. But the
original inspiration of religion as such, in spite of all those
horrible and lamentable distortions, is the yearning for a
contact with *Divine Reality*. This contact has been often lost
or disturbed, but mankind often—consciously or unconsciously
—craved to renew it, craved sometimes for a truer, better,
more adequate religious belief and religious experience.

"La Sua volonta é nostra pace"—"in His will is our peace,"
says Dante. "Our heart is restless till it finds rest in Thee,"
exclaims Augustine. There is no true peace in a poetical, emotional idea or image. We have to reject all kinds of wishful
thinking. We have to believe in God, *because* this is *Truth*—
life-giving Truth. His Reality is something very earnest, very
real: it is the *only true Reality*. And He has to meet us, or
rather we have to meet Him, for He meets us at every step.

PART I

1

Principles of Religious Cognition

1.

Is knowledge necessary in matters of religion, that is, from a *religious point of view?* In other words, is a *conscious contact with Truth* necessary? Could one follow the principle proclaimed by Goethe through the mouth of his Doctor Faust:

> . . . Gefühl ist Alles,
> Name ist Schall und Rauch,
> Umnebelnd Himmelsglut.

("Emotion is everything; names are but sound and smoke, dimming the brightness of Heaven")? Although, even here, a certain knowledge is postulated, as there can be no feelings, no emotions without a certain amount of knowlelge, be it ever so vague and indefinite.

With utmost force Christianity proclaims the redeeming power of Truth and the obligation of man to take a definite conscious attitude towards it and to bear witness thereto: to this *new and decisive Revelation of the Divine Reality,* given in the Son of God, *i.e.,* the Good Tidings. The Johannine aspect of the apostolic message especially (but Paul also) lays stress on Divine Truth and on the revelation of this Truth, on man being enlightened thereby. "And the Life was the *Light* of men, and the Light shines in the Darkness, and the Darkness did not master it . . . There was the true

11

Light, that enlightens every man, coming into the world . . .
The Logos was made flesh and took His abode among us, full
of Grace and Truth . . . For the Law was given through
Moses, but Grace and Truth—it is through Jesus Christ that
they came to be."

In the Johannine Gospel Christ is the Light: "The judgment consists in the fact that Light has come into the world,
but man loved more the Darkness." But to those who become
His disciples, Christ promises that they "will come to know
the Truth and the Truth will make them free." "I am the
Way, and the Truth and the Life!" "I have revealed Thy
Name unto men." "This is Life Eternal that they know Thee,
the only true God, and Him whom Thou hast sent—Jesus
Christ."

We see that Truth and Life, Knowledge and Salvation are
not to be separated according to the Fourth Gospel, yea—
according to the whole apostolic message. That *is Life*: to
know God. Truth is not only "theoretical"; it *makes* free, it
is fulness of Life. So John writes at the end of his First
Epistle: "We know also that the Son of God has come and
has given us light and understanding, that we might know
the true God and we might abide in the True One, in His
Son Jesus Christ. He is the true God and Life Eternal."

There is a thrill running through the apostolic message.
"Now God desires men to discard their ignorance and to
repent"—so the sermon of Paul culminates in Acts 17, on the
Areopagus. The whole message is nothing else than bearing
witness to the conquering and subjugating revelation of God
given in Jesus Christ. The hidden Mystery of God has been
revealed unto us, "the understanding of the Mystery of Christ
which had not been announced to the previous generations of
sons of men, as it now has been revealed." "And to me," so
continues Paul in the Epistle to the Ephesians, "the least
among the saints, is given the grace—to preach to the nations
the unsearchable riches of Christ and to reveal to all what is
the dispensation of the Mystery, which had been from eternity
concealed in God, but *now has been revealed*" (Eph. 3: 4-10).
"He has revealed to us the mysteries of His will according
to His good pleasure": for now the fulness of time has come

and has to be realized, and all things, be it in heaven or on earth, have to be united under One Head, that is Christ (Eph. 1: 8-10).

The documents of the first generations of Christianity are full of the exultant victorious certainty of having come to know the Truth—the Truth which is Life Eternal—not by human means, but through the revelation in the Son of God. "We thank Thee, O Holy Father, for the Life and the Knowledge which Thou hast shown us through Thy Son [Servant] Jesus"—that is the prayer to be pronounced on the eucharistic bread according to the *Teaching of the Twelve Apostles* (*Didache*). And in the prayer after partaking of the food (also in the *Didache*) we read: "We thank Thee, O Holy Father, for Thy Holy name which Thou hast made to dwell in our hearts, and also for the Knowledge, the Faith and the Immortality which Thou hast revealed to us through Thy Son Jesus." Ignatius of Antioch writes: "Ignorance has been abolished, the ancient Kingdom [of the Prince of the World] has been destroyed, when God revealed Himself in the shape of man" (Ignatius, Eph. ch. 19). Martyrs are dying as witnesses of the revealed Truth of God. They must proclaim the Divine Truth which laid hand upon them, and seal it with their blood.

2.

The *claim of religion is to reveal Truth,* to bear witness to Truth. It is the first and fundamental claim. Its aim is not primarily to bring comfort to souls—by preaching beautiful, edifying ideas and hopes. Neither is it primarily in inspiring culture and artistic creation and the highest achievements of human thought by glimpses of a distant, unspeakable Perfection. Rather, it is all that, but it is so *because* this comfort, this beauty, this hope, this creative impulse, this beautifying vision, these glimpses and anticipations of bliss unutterable are based *on a Reality,* because they bear witness to a Reality: to the Divine Reality, to *the* Reality, the only One that really exists, that really possesses the fulness of life. *This* only

makes this comfort, this inspiration a real comfort, a real
inspiration, one that really can satisfy the craving of the heart,
that can really become a source of creative impulse, that can
create and transfigure life. That which is fundamentally false
cannot achieve this. And even if an illusion, a lie could really
comfort the soul and inspire our life and our outlook in a
creative way, it ought to be discarded. True religion cannot
give up its claim to *Truth* as its supreme subject, its supreme
goal and its ultimate inspiration. The Christian religion claims
to bear witness to the ultimate Divine Truth; this was the
purpose of the primitive apostolic message. They had to be
witnesses of the Truth; they could not act otherwise; they
were compelled thereto—and submitted gladly—by the power
of Truth. "We cannot but bear witness of what we have seen
and have heard" (Acts 4: 2). Christians cannot be indifferent
to the question of Truth and Untruth. They must be ready to
die for Truth.

Let us restate this once more. Why need we believe in
God? We have seen it; because this belief in God has proved
helpful and useful in our lives and also in the historical life
of humanity, as the comfort in distress, as the inspiring center
of our existence enhancing its value, hallowing and permeating the texture of life and connecting it with a Background
of Creative Vitality. Religion has given and continues to give
a sense and a meaning to man's life and has inspired man for
his service to his fellow-man and for some of his greatest
achievements in the field of culture and art. One might even
say that there is no real culture without some sort of religion
as its inspiring background. But all this is not the reason why
we should believe in God, for it is only an accessory, not of
a decisive importance. We should be ready to give up all the
advantages of a religious outlook, if it is based on a fundamental untruth or error. The reason it is necessary to believe
in God, the *only* reason which embraces all others, is that
this is Truth. We have to believe in God because this is
Reality, the decisive, fundamental Reality—and *life-giving*
Truth. Only the Truth that really exists, the Divine Truth,
can be truly life-giving, truly fructifying, comforting, restoring and truly creative. But this Truth cannot be proved by

man. It reveals itself by taking hold of man. It is self-revealing, there is no other way to it. The spontaneous Self-Revelation of a Living God who is Truth and Life is the basis of every authentic religious experience.

3.

What is the way to the knowledge of God? What is the essential character of real religious cognition? Of real living Faith?

We have seen that the first factor and agent is God Himself. *He* reveals Himself. His is the initiative. He "knocks at the doors of our heart." He starts the intercourse, He kindles the new life.

This new life of faith, this intercourse with God has to take hold of the whole of man; it makes a demand on all his spiritual forces, on all the elements of his spiritual life, of his personality. The entire man, in the fulness of his spiritual powers, has to give a response to God. Only when my will, my mind, my emotional life, the whole of my personality is "stretching forward" towards Truth, is ready to give a response to the call of Truth, to its "knocking at the door" of my heart, only then can I really get in contact with it, can I attain it, or rather "be attained" thereby. But more than that: there must *be a change,* we must be transformed by the power of Truth. "The Truth will make you free," says the Lord Jesus. "We all, with unveiled face, reflecting as a mirror the glory of the Lord, are transformed into the same image from glory to glory," writes Paul (II Cor. 3: 18).

So this is the characteristic trait of religious cognition, wherein it widely differs from any other sort of knowledge: only by being changed, *transformed* in the deepest of my being can I come to know the Ultimate, the Divine Reality. This is stated with stringent force *e.g.* by a great mystic of the Christian East, Isaac of Syria (7th c.), in the introductory chapter to the collection of his sermons:

Very different is the word of practice from words

of beauty . . . A word proceeding from practice is a
treasure to confide in: but idle wisdom is a pawn of
shame: it is as when an artist paints water on walls
without being able to quench his thirst by it: or as a
man who dreams beautiful dreams.

He who from practical experience speaks about
excellence, brings the word to his hearers as if it were
from the capital won by his commerce: and as from
the stock of his soul, sows his teachings in the ears of
his audience.[1]

The Truth being a Living Truth, my relation to it must
also be living. It must be a growing into the Truth, a being
laid hand upon by the Truth, an organic, progressive union
of the soul with the Truth, a being more and more assimi-
lated thereto. We must become an *organic* member of the
Divine Reality: "I am the Vine, you are the branches"; only
thus can we really come to know it. Those who shout: "Lord,
Lord," and who have even preached His Name and have
worked miracles in His Name but are doers of unrighteous-
ness will be rejected. On the other hand, are we able to approach those unspeakable heights and depths of Divine
Reality and of Divine Wisdom? Only the Spirit of God can
do it. So we have to receive the Spirit of God, we have to
be transfigured by the Spirit of God. There is no other way
to the real knowledge of God! It is only by a painful and
strenuous spiritual growth, by spiritual manly warfare against
my own "old man" and against the powers of Darkness,
under the guidance of the Spirit of God. Only in "newness
of life" can we approach the mysteries of God.

4.

The key to the understanding of the divine mysteries is

[1]See *Mystic Treatises by Isaac of Nineveh,* translated from the Syriac by
A. J. Wensinck (Amsterdam 1923), p. 6. The philosophy of religious cognition of the great Russian religious thinker Ivan Kireyevsky (1806-1856), a
disciple of the Syriac Fathers, is based on this principle.

to be "rooted and grounded in love" (ἐν ἀγάπῃ ἐρριζω-μένοι καὶ τεθεμελιωμένοι, Eph. 3: 17), "strengthened together in love" (συμβιβασθέντες ἐν ἀγάπῃ, Col. 2: 2). Only thus can you arrive to comprehend "what is the width and the length and the height and the depth [of God]" and to "know the love of Christ which transcends all knowledge" (Eph. 3: 18). Only in this way can you attain "the knowledge of God and Christ," in whom are concealed "all the treasures of wisdom and knowledge" (Col. 2: 3). These treasures are revealed to us *only if we grow into Christ, and are really permeated by His Spirit.* But too often Theology is separated from Love! In the same moment as Love is drying up, this Theology—although externally, in its wordings and concepts, remaining correct—loses the intimate link connecting it with its Subject, becomes, according to Paul, "sounding brass or clanging cymbal."

Another important inference to be drawn from this is the "corporate," the "catholic" character of religious knowledge (in the sense of the union of the brethren sharing the same faith and imbibed by the same Spirit under and in the same Lord). It is a knowledge prompted by love which unfolds itself in an atmosphere of love. But "how can man love God whom he has not seen, if he does not love the brother whom he sees?" (I John 4: 20). The promise of His Presence is given "to two or three" gathered in His Name. The knowledge of the mysteries of God, of which Paul speaks, is connected with our being united in Christ: we are all members of One Body, and each member is precious, is of value, even the most humble, the least comely one. We can come to know that "width and length and height and depth" of the mysteries of God only when "rooted and grounded in love, *together with all the saints.*" This is the inspiration and foundation of the Church: the Spirit of Love bringing the brethren together in their standing free, yet linked together in love, before the face of the Divine Reality. I do not approach God alone, but being linked in love with the brethren, as a member of the growing and increasing Body of Christ, this is how, according to the apostolic teaching, we come to know God in His new and decisive revelation—the revelation of His love in His Son—as members of the Church of Christ.

5.

Let us dwell now on the question of proofs. What are the proofs of the Reality which stands behind our faith, the proofs of the reality of God? We have already said there are no external, compulsory proofs. There seem to be so many proofs—through the contemplation of the structure of the universe (the "cosmological"), through the analysis of the idea of God and the meditation thereon (the "ontological"), through listening to the voice of our conscience and to the innermost cravings of the human heart for something Infinite and Transcending (the "psychological" one). But are they sufficient proofs? They are arguments showing the plausibility of Faith, the possibility, yea, if you like, the probability, the likelihood of the existence of God, but no more. They all become a real proof only when they come to signify one thing, which is the only decisive and exhaustive proof: when *God proves Himself*, proves His reality by . . . meeting the soul. He can meet her in the beauty and the amazing and overwhelming grandeur of the structure of the world, He can meet her in the voice of my conscience, and in the craving of my heart for the Infinite—for an infinite Rest, and infinite Satisfaction. He can meet her everywhere: in sorrow and joy, in the happiness of family life, and the cozy warmth of the home, but also in a lonely desert; in search after Truth, and in the vision of Transcendent Beauty, inspiring the great artists. He can meet her, and be met by her—in first place— in the fellow-man, in our active loving compassion for the fellow-man: "Inasmuch as you did it to one of these My brethren even the least, you did it to Me." But all those different experiences of God, of God's reality, mean—in truth—only one thing: that God proves Himself, gives proof of Himself by meeting the soul. Thus, the word of the psalmist is being realized: "Thou hast beset me behind and before, and laid Thine hand upon me" (139: 5). There are striking examples of those encounters with God. God can reveal Himself to the soul even through a bare tree. There is a beautiful story of a young French village-boy who became a novice in a Carmelite monastery in the 17th century. He was rather thick-skulled and not very gifted intellectually, good enough only for kitchen-work and gardening. Once in November on the high-road that ran past the monastery, he saw a tree naturally deprived of its leaves. But suddenly the thought presented itself to his mind, that in spring the tree will again be covered with leaves and blossoms, and sap will run through its branches, and he was struck by a sudden vision of the over-whelming power and majesty of God. He was so deeply shaken and moved in his heart, that from that moment he became a new man—of deepest religious insight and of a burning love for God, a man who was permeated by the sense of God's presence.[2]

To Jacob Böhme after his conversion, the "whole external world with its substance, is a covering of the spiritual world";[3] he feels the presence of God in all creatures, even in herbs and grasses.[4] But especially convincing and the most deeply moving of all these encounters with God in the world which surrounds us are—as we have already said—our encounters with God through and in the fellow-man. When one has known what it is to be in deep distress, alone, seeing no help around, and suddenly a helping hand stretches towards you and a friendly voice speaks comfort and love to you, surely one feels in such a moment that God has spoken, that God is near, that He has revealed Himself through the inter-

---

[2] . . . Il me dit que Dieu lui avait fait une grâce singulière dans sa conversion, étant encore dans le monde, âge de 18 ans. Qu'un jour en hiver, regardant un arbre dépouillé de ses feuilles et considérant que quelque temps après ses feuilles paraîtroient de nouveau, puis des fleurs et des fruits, il reçut une haute veue de la providence et de la puissance de Dieu, qui ne s'est jamais effaciée de son âme: Que cette veue le détacha entièrement du monde et lui donna un tel amour pour Dieu, qu'il ne pouvait pas dire s'il étoit augmenté depuis plus de quarante ans qu'il avait reçu cette grâce." "Entretiens avec le F. Laurent de la Résurrection," in Recueil de Divers Traités de Théologie Mystique (Cologne, 1699), i: "Entretiens," p. 46.

[3] Jakob Böhme, "Von übersinnlichem Leben," 42; cf., e.g. De signatura rerum 9, 1.

[4] "Aurora," X, 57.

mediary of the helping, loving fellow-creature. But it is even
more moving to be given the immense privilege of suddenly
becoming the channel, the bringer, the living representative
of God's active, helping love in relation to one's fellow-man.
The one who helps is sometimes even more innerly shaken
and overwhelmed than the one who receives the benefaction.
"Who am I, O Lord, that Thou dost that through me?" He
feels the presence of the Lord in the suffering brother. It is
one of the highest and most sacred experiences in our life,
something which remains, which moves us ourselves deeply,
awaking not self-complacency, but deepest humility and gratitude. "O Lord, when have we seen Thee hungry and have fed
Thee, or thirsty and have given Thee drink? When have we
seen Thee a stranger and have taken Thee in? Or naked and
clothed Thee? Or when have we seen Thee sick or in prison
and come unto Thee?" And the King shall answer and say
unto them: "Verily I say unto you, inasmuch as you have
done it unto one of the least of these My brethren, you have
done it unto Me." We feel the truth of these words, we feel
His presence behind and in the suffering brother, even the
least of our brethren, often so uninteresting, so average-look-
ing, so helpless, so alone, but—so near to Him, so closely
connected with Him. This is the immanence of the Transcendent God.

The central and decisive encounter of humanity with
God has taken place, according to Christianity, in the coming
of the Lord Jesus. That is the meaning of the Gospel, of
the Good Tidings: "God with us, Emmanuel." An inrush of
God into our life, into history, into the texture of the world's
life. "The Word has been made Flesh . . . and we *have seen*
His Glory." The man born blind, after having been healed,
said: "I believe, O Lord," and "fell upon his face and wor-
shipped Him" (καὶ προσεκύνησεν αὐτῷ, John 9: 38).
"My Lord and My God," says Thomas (John 20: 28).

6.

The whole Gospel story may be considered as a witness

of a *Presence,* of a transcending, sanctifying, unique Presence.
Even more: this is the only way for a Christian to read and
to understand this story, as told by the apostles and witnesses;
it is the sense in which this story has really been told and
written. That is the authentic meaning of this Gospel story.
The "prelude" of the Gospel according to Mark strikes this
keynote: "The beginning of the Gospel of Jesus the Messiah,
the Son of God. As it has been written in Isaiah the prophet:
Behold, I send My messenger before Thy face, which shall
prepare Thy way before Thee. The voice of one crying in the
wilderness: Prepare ye the way of the Lord, make His path
straight" (Mark 1: 1-2). John the Baptist, the great prophet
of repentance, is but the messenger. Somebody Stronger and
Greater than he comes behind him. And John is unworthy
even to stoop down and to unloose the latches of His shoes.
That is the tone which dominates this and the other Gospels.
The whole first chapter of Mark is full of Jesus, proceeding
along the shores of the sea of Galilee and saying to simple
fishermen: "Follow Me"—and they leave all and follow Him
—and healing the sick and preaching the nearness of the
Kingdom. The Kingdom is here—in Him. That is the meaning of the whole story. Something has happened—of decisive,
unique importance, something which kings and prophets were
eager to see, but it was not given to them, and now it has
been revealed, it is here. The words of Isaiah: "The Spirit of
God is upon me, and therefore He has anointed me" . . . are
now being fulfilled. "He began to say unto them: this day is
this scripture fulfilled . . . And all bear witness and wondered
at the words of grace which proceeded out of His mouth"
(Luke 4: 22). Luke especially is full of examples of the
encounter of sinners with the pardoning Lord. But of the
first three Gospels, perhaps Matthew chapter 11 gives the
most condensed expression to the sense of this Presence,
transcending and decisive. "The blind receive their sight and
the lame walk, the lepers are cleansed and the deaf hear, the
dead are raised up and the poor have the good tidings
preached unto them . . ." "Woe unto thee, Chorazin! Woe
unto thee, Bethsaida!"—they have not recognized the Presence, not understood the "mighty works" which have been

done in them. "All things are delivered unto Me of My
Father. Nobody knows the Son but the Father; neither knows
any man the Father but the Son and he to whom the Son will
reveal Him. Come to Me all ye that labor and are heavy
laden, and I will give you rest . . ."

The fifth chapter of Luke—the story of the miraculous
fishing with the words of Peter: "Depart from me, O Lord,
for I am a sinful man!"—is another summit in the manifestation of this sense of an overpowering Presence which permeates the Gospel. And another summit is the story of
Emmaus, how the disciples recognized Him in the breaking
of the bread and said to one another on their way back. "Did
our hearts not burn when He was speaking to us?" And then
the story of the conversion of Zacchaeus, and the woman who
takes hold of the skirt of His mantle, and the centurion who
says to Him: "I am unworthy that Thou shouldst enter my
house, but say one word . . ." and so on: those who came to
Him, sinners, simple folk, sick people, and many others, and
felt His Gracious Presence.

These encounters were decisive during His lifetime on
earth, and afterwards they became the center and essence of
Christian religious experience. This subjugating Presence con-
verted the penitent Saul at the gates of Damascus. It is also
the center of the whole struggle *pro* and *contra*—for and
against the acceptance of God in the thought of one of the
deepest religious writers of modern times, a thinker of an
immense tension and radicalism and profundity: Dostoevsky. Dostoevsky can be considered especially near to us in
our present catastrophic times, full of tragedies and cruel
disappointment, of doubts and misgivings, and also of craving for faith and sometimes also of an immense power of
regenerated faith in God. Dostoevsky's quest for God is
deeply permeated by an undaunted spiritual courage and by
a high-minded and noble radicalism. He does not flinch from
the most decisive, vital and ultimate issues, even if the face
of things sometimes terrifies him. He saw but two issues:
God or godlessness; the others are of no moment. And he
also had the terrific vision of a world which is void—void of
sense, void of God. He has felt what Pascal sometimes felt:

"Le silence de ces espaces infinis m'effraie" ("the silence of
these endless spaces frightens me"). Looking at Holbein's
picture of the maimed body of Christ taken down from the
cross for burial, he shudders. To him Nature seems like a
wild beast tearing to pieces all that we value: it did not even
halt before this One who was the noblest of all that the earth
had ever produced, the crown of the creation. His body was
so mangled and maimed that no hope of His resurrection
would dawn on the mind of those who had seen it. Or rather,
Nature presents itself to our eyes as an immense engine of
newest construction, relentless and regardless in its cold
destructive power, tearing to pieces under its weighty wheels
the highest and the holiest of all that was on earth. So
there is no Justice, no Hope. The immense abyss of the
universe is void. But Dostoevsky's soul cannot accept this. On
the other hand, he is too courageous and honest to turn
his gaze away; he dares to fathom with his eye the depth of
the abyss. This experience, so radical and so genuine, can be
overcome and counterbalanced only by another experience—
as genuine, but more powerful and more subjugating, not
by theories and words. This he found in the person of Jesus
Christ, in His Cross, and in His pardoning mercy, and in the
new life—Life Eternal—streaming forth from Christ. But
Dostoevsky remained honest to the end. He did not want to
sacrifice sincerity. In the famous dialogue of the two brothers
in *Brothers Karamazov* he concentrated all the power of the
atheistic vision, of the atheistic arguments which presented
themselves to his mind. "In the whole of Europe did I not
find such force of atheism as I have embodied in the conversation of the two brothers. Not as a little boy do I believe in
God. My 'Hosanna' has passed through a furnace of doubts."
So he writes in his Notebook. What was the chief point in
this "case of atheism" as expounded by Ivan Karamazov and
what was Dostoevsky's answer? It was the problem of suffering, especially of unjust suffering of innocent people and of
little children. How could one explain it? Can we consider it
as a necessary step towards the future harmony? In that case
I reject this harmony, says Ivan. But perhaps in the Kingdom
of Heaven all will be forgotten and forgiven, and the mother

will press to her heart the murderer of her little child? But this also appears unacceptable to Ivan. The price is too high, we cannot afford it. "In deepest reverence I return the entrance-ticket to the future bliss." It is beyond our means, we cannot pay it. "Not God do I deny, but His world I cannot accept." But that is insurrection! The answer of the other brother—the believing one—is the Cross of Christ. God is not the distant ruler who distributes pains and rewards among men, surveying them from afar, but He Himself has become our companion in suffering. He has descended into the deepest abyss of human distress and dereliction, bearing as man the whole weight of human pains and sorrows unto the death on the Cross. Thus, suffering and even death are sanctified and hallowed through His Presence. The Cross of the Son of God becomes in this way the justification of the plans of God concerning the world. But Ivan makes his last and decisive thrust—in the magnificent, strange and troubling "Legend of the Grand Inquisitor." It is a poem written by him in his student's days. The person of the Grand Inquisitor is Ivan himself, a projection of Ivan's soul. The whole meaning of his long, beautiful, paradoxical and disturbing speech is that the Inquisitor—as Aliosha, the younger brother, suddenly discovers, interrupting the story of Ivan—*does not believe in God.* He loves the image of Christ, he is accustomed to it from his earliest years, he has suffered for His Name, he acts and works in the name of Christ, but he does not believe in Him, he does not believe in God. That is the tragedy of the Grand Inquisitor, the tragedy of Ivan and—more—*the challenge of Ivan.* He too knows the image of Christ, he loves and recognizes its incomparable beauty and grandeur, but *he does not believe* in it. The last word on Ivan's side has been spoken, his heaviest argument has been thrown on the scale. Beautiful, noble and touching is this Image, this Personality; but His teaching is impractical, it does not answer our needs, and thus, Ivan will not believe. He had believed once, now no more. What can be the answer to this? The answer can be only one. In the concluding part of the "Legend" we read: The Prisoner (Christ) has remained silent to all the approaches and invectives of the

Inquisitor. The Inquisitor wants Him to speak. "Say a word, condemn me, curse me, that is more tolerable to me than Thy silence." But the Prisoner does not say a single word. Suddenly He rises in silence, approaches the old man and deposes on the bloodless lips of the nonagenarian a kiss—a kiss of pardon. The Inquisitor is deeply shaken, he turns the key in the lock, opens the heavy door and lets the Prisoner out of the prison into the dark streets of Sevilla. Here Dostoevsky himself speaks through the mouth of Ivan, in this conclusion of the legend. There is *one* answer, *one* proof—and no other proof can be given—the subjugating power of His Presence. *His* Presence and *His* power to forgive, *His* condescending Presence, full of forgiveness, of majesty and mercy, is the answer, the only answer: He Himself meeting our soul.

7.

What is the source and the criterion of faith, the criterion of the ultimate Truth as revealed to us? The answer is: the Spirit of God. Only through God can we come to know God. We have already spoken about this in the previous paragraphs.

Paul writes to the Corinthians: "No man can say that Jesus is the Lord, but by the Holy Spirit" (I Cor. 12: 3). So also the Lord Jesus Himself had said to Peter: "Blessed art thou, Peter Bar-Jona: for not flesh and blood has revealed it to thee, but My Father which is in heaven" (Matt. 16: 17). In the second chapter of his First Epistle to the Corinthians, Paul gives us a deep-going sketch of what we may call Christian epistemology. The riches of God are revealed by the Spirit of God, and only by Him: "For the Spirit searches all things, yea, the depths of God. For what man knows the things of a man, save the spirit of the man which is in him? Even so, the things of God no one knoweth save the Spirit of God. But we received not the spirit of the world, but the Spirit which is of God; that we might know the things that are freely given to us by God. Which things we speak, not

in words which man's wisdom teacheth, but which the Spirit
teacheth . . ." Thus, the preaching of the Good Tidings was
not in the "persuasive words of human wisdom, but in the
demonstration of the Spirit and power."

Let us recapitulate. The Spirit is the bearer and revealer
of the knowledge of God, and the same Spirit is *the source
of sanctity,* it sanctifies those to whom it is given. But this
Spirit—being the Spirit of Love—is given to those who are
united in Love. This, as we already have stated, is the meaning of the Church: to grow together in Love and Truth, as
members of the Body of Christ, being enlightened and permeated by the Spirit. The Spirit of sanctity and love—the
Spirit of God, vouchsafed to the brethren united in love, this
Spirit of God, living in the Church—is the ultimate criterion
of Truth, being Himself the Truth. That is the "witness of
the Spirit," the witness of the Spirit working in the brethren
united by love: there is no other approach to the mysteries
of God. The mystery of Love can be understood only by love!
Of course not by our psychological data, by our natural dis-
positions—but by the breath of Love which is God Himself.

2

Transcendence and Immanence of God

1.

In our experience of God, in the encounter with God, two aspects are intimately linked and complete one another: the sense of the *nearness* and that of the *remoteness* of the Divine, the immanence and the transcendence of God.

The sense of the Holy, causing fear, trembling and reverence, belongs to the core of religious feeling. There is mystery, there is majesty that cannot be investigated by us. An ineffability belongs to the innermost character of the Divine. There is in every religious notion, in every image of divinity—however gross and distorted it may be—a shade of mystery. Sometimes this element is but weakly represented; the Godhead is then more or less felt as dissolved in the life of the world or identified therewith. But often the sense of a transcending Majesty strikes the soul with deepest awe, makes it prostrate itself in humble adoration. Without this awe, without this adoring prostration there is no real piety. The element of "transcendence" is thus to a certain extent present even in immanent or naturalistic aspects of religion. On higher levels it becomes more and more decisive and explicit. "Take off thy shoes from thy feet, for the place whereon thou standest is holy ground"—so the voice of God addresses Moses from out of the burning bush.

This sense of divine aloofness, the being aware of Something that is unapproachable, overpowering, of Something that awakens awe, that requires adoring devotion and surrender, is characteristic of every deeper religious emotion, especially (as we said) on the higher levels of religious life and experience. And this is closely connected with the feeling that the overawing Divinity is at the same time a *Presence* that can be approached, that can be propitiated, that can show Itself gracious and merciful. So Transcendence and Immanence are closely connected with one another in various forms of religious experience. But often one of these elements predominates in a decisive way: in the naturalistic or pantheistic religions, the element of Immanence; in the religious outlook of Platonism, that of Transcendence. In mystical experience—especially in Christian mystical experience—the highest synthesis is achieved between these simultaneously given aspects: the sense of the nearness and the sense of the transcendence of God.

The Highest is quite near, here. He enters my heart and soul. I become united with Him. And Christ, here among us, a man like ourselves ("We have touched Him with our hands," says John), is the inrush of the Living God, of Life Eternal into the texture of our human, earthly life and history: He *is* Life Eternal. "And we have seen His glory," says the apostle, and we worship Him thus with Thomas: "My Lord and my God!"

2.

A striking instance of immanency in religion, where the Transcendent seems to be completely lost sight of, is the religion of Dionysios in ancient Greece. There is a mighty stir and uprush of life in awakening Nature. The young god coming to his worshippers is identified with the wild exultant stream of renewed life. The mountain-tops awake, men and animals revel in the encounter. Nature is entranced and enchanted. Rock and cliffs spout streams of wine, milk flows from the depths of the earth, honey drops from wild forest-oaks. Maenads and wild beasts of the forests join together in an enraptured dance. And the god suddenly appears among them in the shape of a young bull or a he-goat or a young lion, and his raw flesh is torn in pieces and swallowed by his maddened followers. It is the triumph of wild emotions, of savage exuberant life; it is an ecstasy of rioting sap running again through the veins of Nature. There is no transcendency, no moral restraint whatever. The faithful are borne along by this exuberant stream, become part thereof, just little drops, losing their personality, submerged in this torrent of impersonal, elemental, riotous revelry. They are submerged in the Divine, they participate therein, but this Divine is nothing else than the exuberancy of Nature-life, always renascent from death and always succumbing to it anew. For in pure Immanence there is no victory over death. This young god himself, carried along in triumph, succumbs to it again and again. There is no final redemption from the sway of Fate and Evil and Suffering and Death in the purely immanent divinities of Nature.

Alongside the wild Dionysian cult which streamed into Greece in comparatively recent times (7th or 8th century B.C.) from half-barbarian Thracia, there is the balanced, harmonious Olympian Greek religion, with its beautiful, so human, so nobly shaped gods, in whose company even the turbulent Dionysios became harmonized, a vision of shining youthful beauty and grace. Those divinities of the Olympian pantheon are not—or are no more, if they ever had been—an embodiment of elemental forces of Nature; they are shapes of beauty, they are inspired by an aesthetic conception of life, they reign in a universe of harmony and beauty. But in the aesthetic character of their universe lies its weakness.

The aesthetic point of view obscures the moral one. There is harmony and balance, but no final justice in this world. And no salvation from death. Death swallows up all individuals and all that is concrete and personal, human joys and human sorrows, this man and that man, this plant and that plant—only the species remains, only the general outlines, the harmony and the order. And the gods are the guardians thereof. They are "jealous" of all individual achievements, of all that brings man near to immortality: they keep immortality for themselves. They are the embodiments of the unshakable laws of the universe, where all that is individual passes, but the laws remain. Their beauty, their shining forms are immanent to the immutable harmony and order of the "Cosmos" that passes away in all its components, except the immortal gods, but remains in its general outlines, in its eternal beauty and life. But it is a life composed of innumerable series of deaths, not victorious over Death, not conquering and destroying it, not really transcendent to it—no real Life Eternal. These gods are immanent in the beauty and harmony of an unsatisfactory "Cosmos," unsatisfactory despite all its beauty: because it is dying, decaying, and remaining only in its idea, in its general forms and unshaken order. The stoic on the imperial throne, Marcus Aurelius, having praised the beauty and harmony of the world's order, suddenly exclaims in a fit of deepest despondency: "How long then?" And six hundred years before, another sage—the great Heraclitus— also, after entranced, enthusiastic words about the order and harmony of universal life, adds in deepest sadness and resignation: "The most beautiful universe is comparable to a heap of rubbish scattered about at random." On the line of pure immanence there is release from the bonds of individuality, but no final release from the fetters of Death. All that is concrete and individual, all living personality, is vowed to Death.

3.

The transcendent God! An immense truth is revealed here, as we have seen it already. The Seraphim in the vision of Isaiah (ch. 6) cover their faces with their wings and exclaim in fear and trembling: "Holy, holy, holy is the Lord Sabaoth!" The creature does not dare to look up. This sense of overwhelming, crushing Majesty and of immense distance between God and creature pervades the writings of the prophets. There are words, there are prayers or confessions which, to a certain extent, succeed in conveying this sense of immense distance—the utter smallness and nothingness of the creature and the overpowering greatness of God: of God who is Master over life and death, over being and non-being, over all that exists and whatsoever shall come into existence, but is still beyond that, Unreachable, Unfathomable, Unspeakable—Real, the Only One who is really Real in the ultimate sense of the word.

The transcending majesty of God is strongly conveyed, for example, in the fortieth chapter of Isaiah:

> Who hath measured the waters in the hollow of his hand, and meted out heaven with the span, and comprehended all dust of the earth in a measure, and weighed the mountains in scales, and the hills in a balance?
>
> Who hath directed the Spirit of the Lord, or being his counsellor hath taught him?
>
> With whom took he counsel, and who instructed him, and taught him in the path of judgment, and taught him knowledge, and shewed to him the way of understanding?
>
> Behold, the nations are as a drop of a bucket, and are counted as the small dust on the balance: behold, he taketh up the isles as a very little thing.
>
> And Lebanon is not sufficient to burn, nor the beasts thereof sufficient for a burnt offering.
>
> All nations before him are as nothing; and they are counted to him less than nothing, and vanity.
>
> To whom then will ye liken God? or what likeness will ye compare unto him?
>
> . . . Have ye not known? have ye not heard? hath it not been told you from the beginning? have ye not understood from the foundations of earth?
>
> It is he who sitteth upon the circle of the earth, and the inhabitants thereof are as grasshoppers; that stretcheth out the heavens as a curtain, and spreadeth them out as a tent to dwell in;
>
> That bringeth the princes to nothing; he maketh the judges of the earth as vanity.
>
> Scarcely they have been planted; scarcely they have been sown; scarcely their stem did take root in the earth; and he shall blow upon them, and they shall

wither, and the whirlwind shall take them away as
stubble.

To whom then will ye liken me, or shall I be equal?
saith the Holy One.

Lift up your eyes on high, and behold who hath
created these things, that bringeth out their host by
number: he calleth them all by names by the greatness
of his might, for that he is strong in power; not one
faileth (vv. 12-18 and 21-26).

"I am Alpha and Omega, the Beginning and the Ending,
saith the Lord, which is, and which was, and which is to
come, the Almighty"—so we read in the Revelation of St.
John.

The Divine Darkness, the Primordial Light, so bright that
it is felt as darkness by our bedazzled eyes which are too
weak to sustain it, the Divine Desert, or Waste, the Unknown
Country, the Abyss of Divine Silence ("in which are engulfed
all the true lovers," says Ruysbroeck), the totally Other
("Niti! Niti!"—"Not so! Not so!"—of the Upanishads), the
Night of Otherness and total Estrangement, of which John
of the Cross exclaims in rapture:

> O Noche que guiaste!
> O Noch' amable mas que l'alborada! . . .

("O Night, that hast led me! O Night, that art more
lovable than the light of the dawn!")—these all are but
utterly inadequate images, poor stammerings pointing to the
overwhelming Majesty of Transcendent Reality and Life.
Unapproachable Transcendence, unfathomable depth of pro-
foundest Peace and Quiet which is also utterly dynamic; there
is no lifelessness, no passivity, but Creative Energy, Overpowering Might. Burning, cleansing, attracting, opening the
eyes of the soul, converting, taking hold of, totally reshaping,
changing, making a new creature. The Transcendent God
shows His Transcendence, His Otherness, His overpowering,
indescribable Majesty in His Immanence, in His drawing near,
in His speaking to the heart.

4.

"Lo! I stand at the door and I knock. And if any man hears My voice and opens to Me I will come to him, and sup with him, and he with Me." The Overpowering, the Transcendent is near—that is mystical experience. In this mystical experience the Immanence of the Transcendent—as we said already—becomes apparent. The nearer it comes, the greater His incomparable Majesty reveals itself to us. And the summit of His power and majesty is revealed just in this, His drawing near, in His condescension, in His pouring Himself out in love. This is the real, the ultimate sense of His Immanence: His pouring Himself out in love.

The Immanence is also revelation of His unique greatness, of His uniqueness: He sustains us, He encloses us from all sides. All live only through Him and by Him. His is the working power, His the source of life which permeates all. "In Him we live and move and exist," says St. Paul, repeating the words of a stoic poet. A rightly understood immanency does not exclude a rightly understood transcendence in the notion of God, rather they presuppose and complete each other. There is no true religious experience where one of these two aspects of religion is lacking. We can see it in the Old Testament, but especially in the Christian revelation. In chapter forty of Isaiah, already quoted, where the incomparable power and transcending majesty of God were depicted, we see both aspects stressed with equal strength:

> Behold, the Lord God will come with strong hand, and his arm shall rule for him: behold, his reward is with him, and his work before him.
>
> He shall feed his flock like a shepherd: he shall gather the lambs with his arm, and carry them in his bosom, and shall gently lead those that are with young. . . .
>
> . . . Why sayest thou, O Jacob, and speakest, O Israel; my way is hidden from the Lord, and my judgment is passed over from my God?

Hast thou not known? hast thou not heard? that
the everlasting God, the Lord, the Creator of the ends
of the earth, fainteth not, neither is weary? there is
no searching of his understanding.

He giveth power to the faint; and to them that
have no might he increaseth strength (vv. 10, 11,
27-29).

And compare in chapter 42 these two closely connected
verses (15-16), of which the first depicts the awe-inspiring,
dreadful power of the Lord, whose Presence burns and shakes
the created world to its foundations, and the next, imme-
diately following one stresses the condescending meekness
and kindness of the same Lord:

I will make waste mountains and hills, and dry up
all their herbs; and I will make the rivers islands, and
I will dry up the pools . . .

And I will bring the blind by a way that they know
not; I will lead them in paths that they have not
known: I will make darkness light before them, and
crooked things straight. These things will I do unto
them, and not forsake them.

The Old Testament knows that the Lord surrounds us
from all sides; that He speaks to us through the voice of the
creation:

Thou has beset me behind and before, and laid
thy hand upon me . . . Whither shall I go from thy
spirit? or whither shall I flee from thy presence?

If I ascend up into heaven, thou art there; if I make
my bed in hell, behold, thou art there.

If I take the wings of the morning, and dwell in
the uttermost depths of the sea;

Even there shall thy hand lead me, and thy right
hand shall hold me. (Psalm 139: 5, 7-10).

The heavens declare the glory of God; and the
firmament sheweth his handy work. (Psalm 9: 1).

God's nearness, God's presence can dawn on us from different quarters, from different events and experiences of our life. We can hear His voice in the warmth and the sanctity of the family hearth, in the tenderness of domestic affections, in happiness and joy, in the blissful atmosphere of family love, but also in sorrowful visitations, in pain and suffering. We feel His Presence in the voice of our moral conscience, in the inspiration which incites us to deeds of heroic self-sacrifice. In the beauty of heroic self-abnegation, in the perseverance of long silent hours of courageous suffering born for His sake, His nearness is felt. We feel it, as we have already seen, especially when we try to alleviate the suffering of our brethren: "I was hungry and you gave Me to eat; I was thirsty, and you gave Me to drink; I was naked and you clothed Me; I was homeless, and you took Me in your house; I was sick and in prison, and you came to Me . . ." "Because you did it to one of the least of these My brethren, you have done it unto Me." He is the living background on which these our brethren stand and live. When they suffer, His mystical Presence in them, through them, behind them becomes especially apparent.

Not only those brethren can be deeply touched and moved when a saving hand is stretched out to them, not only *they* feel then the nearness of the saving and helping Lord in this helping brotherly hand, in this deed of brotherly love which saves them and cheers them up, but as we said, in a far greater measure *we,* if we are the helping ones—if this help, this saving deed is being accomplished through us, if we become the channel, so to say, of this saving action towards our brethren—much more we—I say—may receive the great boon, the great grace of feeling His Presence, that suddenly reveals itself to us in the suffering brethren. Not that the brother becomes by himself uninteresting to us, not that his individuality is, so to say, merged into or swallowed up for us by the Presence of the Divine. Just the contrary: this human concrete individuality of the least of our brethren whom we are actively helping becomes precious to us: it is enlightened, is illuminated for our spiritual eye by the Presence of Christ in this, perhaps the least one, the least interest-

ing and inspiring one, our suffering brother. This is the
Christian immanence of Divine Love, this is what makes the
person of the least of our brethren so sacred, this is what
gives to authentic Christian love a *mystical tone*: the sense
of the nearness, of the Presence of the Lord. This is one—
and perhaps the most telling and convincing one—of the real
mystical encounters between God and the Christian soul.

5.

We have said already: the outstanding, striking feature
of the mystical experience, of the mystical encounter between
God and the soul at its height is the most intimate union of
Divine Transcendence with Divine Immanence. Here, present,
"taking hold of me," "laying His hand on me," more: the
Fount of my being, felt by me as such (the "Root of Life,"
according to Plotinus), my Lord and my King and my Master,
the Precious Pearl of the soul—and at the same time Unfathomable and Unutterable Majesty, the Transcending Light
that dazzles, the Fire that consumes all that is unclean, that
makes the creature kneel down in silent adoration. "Take
off thy shoes from off thy feet, for the place whereon thou
standest is holy ground!"

"Engradeceis vuestra nada!" says Teresa of Spain ("Thou
fill'st with grace this Nothing!"). "Feu" ("Fire"): so begins
the "document" of Pascal, written by him in the night of his
conversion. "O lámparas de fuego" ("O flashes of fire!"),
exclaims John of the Cross.

The central experience of the Christian mystic (but we
find this also in theistic mystical experience outside of Christianity, for instance, in Persia and medieval India) is that
the High One, the Supreme One voluntarily and freely con-
descends, "stoops down" to come to me, to fill up the chasm
between His Majesty and Glory and my nothingness. And this
enhances my feeling of admiring gratitude, my sense of being
overwhelmed, being laid hand upon by the boundless Love.
"Who art Thou, O my sweetest God (*O dulcissime Deus
meus*), and who am I, the little servant and worm before Thy

face?" says Francis of Assisi. "I am not worthy that Thou shouldst enter under the roof of my house": so speaks the soul in the eucharistic prayers, in the East and the West, before Communion.

The condescending humility and lovingkindness of the Almighty God: that is the keynote of Christian mystical experience and Christian piety. That is also the whole contents, the whole purport of the Christian message, of the witness of the apostles.

6.

"We have seen . . . His *Glory*." "We have touched with our hands"—and That was "the Life Eternal." Immanence and Transcendence given simultaneously: this is based on a fact, and this fact is: the Word among us, manifested in Flesh, having become Flesh—most intimate fusion or rather synthesis of Transcendence and Immanence, but not only in our interior experiences and emotions, but in *a fact,* in that which has really taken place. "We have heard and seen and touched it with our hands . . . and we bear witness thereof," and that was "the Life Eternal." The salvation of the world lies in the fact that Transcendent God became Man, became near to me and like me, and that we are now "grafted" on Him. Not only did He condescend, but now our poor Humanity is grafted on His Divinity in order that it should share in His Transcendence and Glory.

3

Some Problems of the History of Religions

RELIGIOUS EXPERIENCE IN THE OLD TESTAMENT

1.

There are different approaches to the fact of the existence of a great variety of religions, widely differing from one another not only in their external forms of worship, but also in their whole outlook and in their spiritual and moral value. There is, *e.g.*, a point of view (we could perhaps call it "ultra-calvinistic") that denies the existence of any positive trait in the fallen nature of man and therefore also in all heathen religions. On the other hand there is an approach that we could call "relativistic." When it is connected with a certain general belief in God, it considers all the so-called "higher" religions as more or less equal in their ultimate value—as equally valuable and acceptable approaches to the mystery of the Divine. This point of view is now often preached by the adepts of theosophy. It is also shared by a number of Indian religious thinkers. A typical example thereof is the prayer of the philosopher Abul-Fasl (1547-1595), who lived at the court of the great emperor of India, the "Great Mogul" Akbar.[1] He feels the presence of God in an equal way in the mosque, in heathen temples, in Buddhist communities, in Christian and Jewish worship.

But there is also another kind of relativistic approach to

religion that is based on an agnostic or essentially atheistic outlook and considers all religions purely as a projection of the human mind and therefore totally subject to the laws of human evolution. Sometimes combined therewith—by what right?—is a very optimistic appraisal of this evolution as a continuous ascension of man to higher (only psychologically, subjectively higher, if there is no Absolute Divine Reality corresponding to them) forms of belief and moral consciousness.

This evolutionary theory has many very different aspects. It can be "positivistic," as with Auguste Comte (1798-1857) and his followers: religion according to him is only a necessary step in the evolution and growth of the human mind towards its goal, scientific knowledge; it has therefore to be superseded by the higher phase, the scientific one, and has therefore no claim to any permanent value. But there are other evolutionary theories that attach or seem to attach a certain intrinsic value (not only that of a transitory step towards scientific knowledge) to some higher forms of religion and religious experience. But this is possible only on the basis of recognition (implicit or outspoken) of the fundamental truth of religion—the existence of a Divine Reality. Otherwise it would be senseless. A purely historical and relativistic approach excludes any judgment of value, gives no right whatever for such a judgment. If all religion has no foundation in a Supreme Reality and is essentially an error, then all the differences in the evaluation of the different aspects of religion have merely a psychological, purely subjective base. We have no right then to speak of any *progressive* evolution (or only in the sense of Auguste Comte—see above). We can only *describe* successive phases, abstaining from every judgment of value.

Quite different is the position of one who believes in the Supreme Divine Reality. In the light of this Supreme Divine Truth everything can and must be weighed and tested as to its relation thereto. A judgment of value can therefore be formed concerning all the forms and aspects of human belief and religion.

2.

What is the Christian, the apostolic attitude in relation to the religious quest and religious belief of mankind outside the revelation of the Old and the New Testament?

This attitude is *double*. It is stated clearly enough in chapter 17 of the Book of Acts. Paul is described as being "anguished" in his spirit in seeing the city of Athens "full of idols" (κατείδωλον). And he speaks to a small cultivated audience on the Areopagus hill. He has found among other shrines in Athens an altar dedicated to the "Unknown God." This God he will preach to them. This God, Creator of the world, does not dwell in temples; He has created the human race, "setting up certain periods and boundaries for their abode, that they should seek Him, in the hope that they might attain Him and find Him, though indeed, He is not far from each one of us." And Paul continues: "Because in Him we live and move and exist. As some of your poets have said: 'For we are also of His race.'" (Both these last sentences are quotations from Greek religious writers.) Likewise in the Prologue to St. John's Gospel we read: "There was the true Light that enlightens every man (ὃ φωτίζει πάντα ἄνθρωπον) coming into the world." The meaning of the two passages—the words of Paul and this sentence from St. John's Gospel (1:9)—is that there is a certain knowledge of God or a yearning and craving and searching after Him given to all men, even in the heathen world. In accordance therewith are the words of Paul in chapters 1 and 2 of Romans concerning the possibility of a certain knowledge of God as Divine Creator open to all men through the contemplation of the works of creation and concerning the interior moral code written in the hearts of men (1:19-20, 2:14-15). That would coincide with what two early Christian Fathers —Justin the Philosopher and Clement of Alexandria—say of the seed of the Divine Logos scattered in the hearts of the just among the Greeks, thus in the hearts of Socrates and Heraclitus. There is a natural leaning in man, innate to man, towards God: it is the working of the Divine Logos who gives

light and life. Man is naturally attracted by the Divine Logos
who is the interior Law according to which the world has its
being. And this explains the glimpses of truth and of genuine
knowledge of God scattered in the "heathen" religions . . .
among heaps of the grossest errors and moral degradation.

For there is also another aspect of paganism that is stressed
with no lesser force in the apostolic message and in the
experience and conviction of primitive Christianity: paganism
as the religion of man who has lost the true knowledge of
God, the religion of fallen man. It has become a *false religion,* and more than that: it has become the playground of
antigodly, of *demonic, evil powers.* This point of view is
stressed with utmost energy by the same St. Paul in his First
and Second Epistles to the Corinthians: "What they (the
pagans) sacrifice, they sacrifice to demons and not to God. I
do not want you to become partners with demons. You
cannot drink the cup of the Lord and the cup of the demons.
You cannot partake in the Lord's supper and in the meal of
the demons" (I Cor. 10: 20, 22). "Is there a fellowship
between light and darkness? Is there a concord between Christ
and Belial? . . . Can there be an agreement between the
temple of God and the idols? For we are the temple of the
living God." . . . (I Cor. 6:14-16).

And this is not purely theoretical assertion, it is the result
of the strong feeling and conviction of the first Christians
that in pagan worship they were faced with something
morally perverse and demonic. It was a deeply felt experience
of the early Christians that something hostile and substantially
evil faced them in the pagan cults. And there were sufficient
reasons for this.

3.

Anyone who has been attentively studying different aspects
and phases of the world religions outside the religions of the
Old and New Testament cannot help being struck by the
deep-going fundamental *duality* that permeates this religious
development. The contrasts are great and striking. Alongside

beautiful hymns to the Supreme God and a religious craving
for the One Absolute Divinity which inspire especially some
ancient Indian and Egyptian texts, we have the motley pantheon of popular religion and sometimes—so, *e.g.,* in some
Babylonian texts and in later Hellenism—the sense of the all-
pervading presence and the immense power of innumerable
evil spirits, a real "polydemonism" that fills the heart with
terror. The best means to protect oneself are magical rites
and incantations. This sense of horror permeates, *e.g.,* the
famous Assyro-Babylonian incantation-text agains the Evil
Seven:

> They are Seven! They are Seven!
> In the depth of the Ocean they are Seven,
> They are Seven roaming through the Heaven,
> They are neither male nor female,
> They are like the roaring wind . . .
> They don't know compassion or mercy,
> They don't listen to prayer or supplications . . .
>
> The First among them is the Southern Wind,
> The Second—the Dragon with wide-open jaws
> Whom nobody can resist,
> The Third is the ferocious Leopard
> Who swallows children,
> The Fourth is the terrible Snake . . .
>
> They bring along darkness from city to city,
> Storms that make Heaven tremble,
> Thick cloud that plunges Heaven into darkness . . .
>
> They are crawling like snakes on their belly,
> They are howling like a pack of hounds,
> Through the highest wall and through the thickest wall
> They pass like ravening storm,
> Bursting into one house after another,
> No door can detain them,

No lock can stop them,
For over the threshold they crawl in like a Serpent . . .[1]

and so on.

On the other hand what immense religious dynamism is sometimes to be found in the old texts of a monotheistic (or pantheistic) inspiration from Egypt or ancient India! I will make only a few quotations from some old Egyptian documents. An old pyramid text speaks of Him "who is without name, whose name is hidden." Or there is a papyrus from Leyden (19th dynasty) that recognizes in the god Amon a manifestation of the Supreme Divinity: "No god knows His real aspect . . . He has no image that could be designed . . . He is too full of mystery for His glory to be revealed, too great to be scrutinized, too mighty to be known . . ." This tradition continues also in later times. On the entrance of the Ptolemaic temple of Medumoud there is the following inscription: "The One Who has produced Himself, Whose name is secret and Who hides Himself from His children, Who raised His head out of the dark abyss, Who has existed when there was nobody except Him. Who rose alone, given birth to Himself, according to Whose designs all beings have been produced, the Unknown as to His image, Who hides Himself from His creation . . ." In the like way the God Ptah is called (in the texts coming from Memphis) "Father of all the gods, the great God of the primordial times," the "Lord of the Years," the "Master of Eternity."[2]

And now let us turn to some texts from ancient India. There is a strain of deep-felt, most earnest and striking religious yearning, religious "nostalgia" that runs through many passages of the Upanishads and of related texts (as the Mokshadhârma of the Mahâbhâratam), a proclaiming of the One, the only One that really exists, the "Satya Satyasya" ("the Reality of the Reality").[3] "For there is Something or

[1]The text of this prayer is given in René Grousset's *Histoire de l'Asie*, vol. 1 (1922), pp. 225-26.

[2]Quoted by Desroches-Noblecourt in his article "Les religions égyptiennes," in the great collective work *Histoire générale des religions*, ed. Maxime Gorce and R. Mortier, vol. 1 (Paris, 1948), pp. 252, 215.

[3]Brihad-Aran. Up. 2, 1, 20. Cfr. Oltramare, *Histoire des idées théo-*

Someone that does not grow old, the Ancient, the Eternal One,"[4] "that exists by Himself," something "immortal, permanent," "not subject to changes,"[5] "great, free from disease,"[6] "radiant and immutable,"[7] that is "beyond hunger and thirst, beyond sorrow and error, beyond old age and death."[8] "His name is 'High,' because He is raised high above all evil."[9] He is the Ineffable, Unfathomable One, "the deep Hidden One, Who can neither be seized by thought nor measured,"[10] of Whom the only thing that can be said is: "He is!"[11] and "Who alone really exists."[12] In Him we have the true refuge,[13] He is the longed-for "shore," beyond all sorrow.[14] "To know Him is 'the goal of the Upanishads' "[15] "His name is: 'The One Whom we yearn for.' "[16] "Who has come to know Him becomes wise, and in search of Him, the ascetics start on their wanderings, in nostalgia for a better land." "Having come to know Him, brahmins cease to desire sons, possessions, worlds, and like beggars they enter a homeless life."[17] For of Him it is said: "The Infinite is bliss. There is no bliss in what is finite. Only in the Infinite there is bliss."[18] And again: "Brahma is bliss."[19] And from many passages of these ancient texts we hear these accents of joy:

sophiques dans les Indes (Annales du Musée Guimet, Bibliotheque d'Etudes vol. 23, 1902), pp. 75, 115.

[4]Cvetâcv. Up. 3, 21; *Sacred Books of the East*, vol. 15, p. 248.

[5]Mokshadhârma Adh. 206, 32, Adh. 179, 25; Deussen, *Vier philosophische Texte des Mahâbhâratam* (1906), pp. 232, 134.

[6]I 43, 71; *Vier philosophische Texte* . . . p. 22.

[7]Prasna Up. 4; see Hildebrand, *Aus Brahmânas und Upanishaden* (1921), p. 147.

[8]Brihad-Aran. Up. 5, 5, 1.

[9]Chandog. Up. 1, 6, 7.

[10]Maitr. Up. 5; Taittir. Up. 2, 91. Cfr. Oltramare, p. 74.

[11]Kâth. Up. 6, 12.

[12]See J. Dalman, *Nirvana: Eine Studie zur Vorgeschichte des Buddhismus* (1896), p. 54 ff. with quotations from Mahâbhâratan.

[13]Mokshadhârma Adh. 206, 32; *Vier philosophische Texte* . . . p. 239.

[14]Chandog. Up. 7, 1, 3.

[15]Cvetâcv. Up. 1, 6; Deussen, *Sechzig Upanishaden des Veda*, p. 294.

[16]Ken. Up. 321; *ibid.* p. 208.

[17]Brihad-Aran. Up. 3, 5, 4, 4, 22. Cfr. H. Oldenberg, *Die Lehre der Upanishaden und die Anfänge des Buddhismus* (1915), p. 139.

[18]Chandog. Up 7, 23; *Sacred Books of the East*, vol. 1, p. 123.

[19]Taittir. Up. 3, 6. Cfr. Taittir. Up. 2; Mund. Up. 2, 2, 7.

"He that has come to know Him has attained freedom; he that has come to know Him has attained peace; he that has come to know Him becomes immortal!"[20] Or listen to this passage, also from the Kâtha-Upanishad: "The wise man who by means of meditation on the Âtman (the Self) recognizes the Ancient Who is difficult to be seen, Who has entered into the dark, Who is hidden in the cave, Who dwells in the abyss as God—he indeed leaves joy and sorrow far behind for ever."[21]

But this Ultimate Reality is conceived by the authors of the Upanishads as an impersonal Divine Ocean, in which all is engulfed, as a Divine Indifference beyond all our distinctions, not as a loving creative personality. "Tat tvam âsi"— "That is you"—that is the formula of deliverance: to conceive all being as *one* and individualisation as false, as the "nightmare" by which is chained the One Supreme Being. There is therefore a breath of cold indifference about this Divine all-permeating Substance: it takes no interest in any individual being; it is neither a loving Father nor a merciful Savior. And also on the other hand, alongside these glimpses of a higher Divine Reality, alongside an experience thereof, what strange absurdities, gross magical practices, strange, poor and primitive cosmological speculations verging on magic are piled up in the same texts! The dynamism of a deep religious craving and an intense religious quest, the wonderful glimpse of the Supreme Reality remain here mixed up with strata of much lower religious conceptions that are so characteristic of the religions of India. Both elements are characteristic—the higher yearnings and experiences and the superstition and magic pervading the popular religion. And likewise what a strange and motley impression the official religions of Egypt make upon us with the multiplicity of their magical rites, their cults of animals, their magical texts concerning the life beyond the grave and the multitude of their gods—with a monotheistic (or rather henotheistic[22]) strain here and there making its

[20]Kâth. Up. 3, 15, 17; 5, 13, 6 and 9; Brihad-Aran. Up. 4, 4, 7, 19, 17; Chandog. Up. 2, 23, 2; Keda. Up. 12-13, and many similar passages.
[21]Kâth. Up. 1, 2, 12.
[22]This term has been introduced by the great scholar in Indology and the

way, or rather losing itself among the floods of grosser practices and conceptions.

4.

There is a law in the history of religion not always sufficiently paid attention to by historians of religion: the simultaneous presence of elements of very different religious value. Sometimes a sudden *breaking through* of a higher conception takes place, felt as a sudden glimpse of, a sudden contact with a Higher Reality—the Divine Reality amidst the rubbish and trash of often morally repulsive and even ludicrous polytheistic and polydemonistic conceptions. The classical example is that of the Bushmen of South Africa (dating from the 19th century), referred to by Andrew Lang in his famous books *Myth, Ritual and Religion* (2nd edition, 1906) and *The Making of Religion* (1898). They worship as their chief deity a strange being called Kagn, represented as a gigantic ichneumon (something between a weasel and a lizard). All kinds of lascivious and strange stories of his mating with different animals, queer kinds of love-stories are being told of this repulsive divinity. But when a European (who had spent many years among the Bushmen and knew how to approach them) asked a Bushman what they were doing when hunting in the desert, far from home, having no luck and their provisions being exhausted. The Bushman answered, "Well, they pray to Kagn." And how do they pray?—"Kagn, Kagn! Are we not your children? Don't you see our hunger? Help us!"[23] The notion of a merciful Supreme Father suddenly dawns upon their conscience amidst all this trash of inept mythological images.

Another example of this sudden *breaking through* of a higher conception or rather a higher experience of God is

comparative study of religion Prof. Max Müller to designate a temporary monotheistic mood, a temporary exaltation of some god, to whom one just happens to pray, as the only one who counts for you at the time.

[23]A. Lang, *The Making of Religion*, p. 210. Cfr. Orpen, "A Glimpse into the Mythology of the Malvti Bushmen," *Cape Monthly Magazine*, July, 1874.

that of the great sage and preacher of a moral religion
Epictetus (2nd century A.D.). For him God is theoretically
the pantheistical soul of the universe according to the stoic
conception. It is Universal Law and Harmony, but not a living
Divine Person, the Living God with Whom one can have a
moral contact of person to person. And nevertheless there are
prayers and invocations addressed by Epictetus to this God
(generally conceived as the immutable Law of Nature) full
of a real burning of the soul, and—what is more—this God
appears then suddenly as the bountiful Father of All, before
Whom the soul bows in deepest trust and devotion.

Another striking contradiction can be found in the Hinayâna Buddhism (Buddhism "of the Little Ferry"). Ancient
Buddhist psychological and philosophical texts deny the
existence of a soul-substance as also that of any higher Reality. It is the "thirst" for existence (which is the root of the
painful, endless series of rebirths!) that holds together the
separate elements of the human person and of any individual
being. When this "thirst" is overcome, the elements fall
asunder and the ultimate salvation from suffering (the supreme aim of the Buddhist preaching), Nirvâna ("extinction"), is reached. From this point of view Nirvâna can really
mean nothing else than total extinction. This is the natural
and necessary deduction from these theoretical presuppositions. So much the more as—as we already have said—any
absolute and ultimate Divine Reality is *ignored* by this aspect
of Buddhism.[24] More than that: often the existence of an
absolute, immutable Reality is emphatically denied (or seems
to be so). "Forasmuch, O disciples," so Buddha is reported
to have said, "as there cannot be in truth discovered the
existence either of a spiritual reality or of anything proper
to it, is not therefore the belief that says: 'this is the world
and that is the "Self,"[25] this shall I become after death: firm,
permanent, eternal, immutable, and this shall I remain in
eternity,' is this belief not simply silly nonsense?" "How can
such a faith be anything else than silly nonsense, O Lord,"

[24]Not so in the Mahayâna—the Buddhism "of the Great Ferry" (or:
"Vehicle").

[25]*Atta*—in Sanskrit: *Atman*.

comes the answer.[26] Therefore the Buddhist texts designate the Nirvâna sometimes as total disappearance, total cessation, the non-existent, the abolition of will, the disolution,[27] the total departure in which nothing is left.[28] So the nun Kisa Gotami, beholding once how in the convent all the lights were extinguished and then lit again, was filled with spiritual comfort and exclaimed: "Similar to these lights are the living beings; they go out and then again they light up. But those who have obtained Nirvâna are not seen any more."[29]

In the last stage of Nirvâna "all forms of existence disappear totally," "any way to existence is destroyed."[30] But that is not the only explanation of Nirvâna. There are many texts of an agnostic tinge; Buddha (or his followers) simply refuse to say whether Nirvâna means a sort of new existence— unutterable, undescribable—or the total cessation of all, even highest sort of existence. And then there are suddenly texts (and not a few of them) where Nirvâna is spoken of in mystical tones: as the highest blissful state, unspeakable, utterly transcending, but possessing the highest positive contents, not only the negative one—of cessation of pain. Characteristic is the conversation of the famous German historian of religion and religious philosopher Rudolph Otto during his stay in Ceylon, the center of "classical" (this designation ought now to be given up) *i.e.,* Hinayâna Buddhism, with a very learned, intellectually refined Buddhist monk. Quoting many texts he exposed to Otto the doctrine to which he firmly adhered, of the total non-existence of the soul and of any ultimate spiritual substance. But when asked by Otto "what then is Nirvâna?", he suddenly grew silent and then murmured with an enraptured smile only these two words: "Bliss unspeakable!" And in fact, if we turn again to ancient Bud-

[26]Alagaddûpama Sutta, Majjh. Nik. no. 22. Cfr. Oldenberg, *Buddha* (7th ed.), pp. 314-15.

[27]See quotations in Warren, *Buddhism in Translations,* p. 372; V. Kojevnikov, *Buddhism Compared to Christianity* (in Russian, 1916), vol. 2, p. 700; J. Dalman, *Nirvana* . . . p. 9.

[28]Words of Buddha to his disciple Ananda in Mahaparin. Sutta 3, 20; 4, 37-42; 5, 5; *Sacred Books of the East,* vol. 3, pp. 117, 146, 153-59.

[29]Dhammapada-Atthakatha.

[30]Itivattaka 44; trans. by Karl Schmidt, *Die Erlösung von Leiden: Ausgewählte Reden des Buddha* (Munich, 1921), vol. 2, p. 91.

dhist texts, even of the so-called "classical" Hinayâna Buddhism (for in the Mahayâna—"Great Ferry"—Buddhism
which developed later, we have a most explicit positive religious outlook, with Buddha as the divine center thereof), we
meet with many definitions of Nirvâna of a *positive* character;
some of them at least cannot be explained solely as the expression of joy over the cessation of suffering and the stopping
of the painful "wheel" of endless rebirths through total
"extinction." Some of them at least point to a definite *mystical*
conception of Nirvâna as being uplifted into something unspeakable but positively blissful (as this monk told Otto)
and transcending. This philosophy of salvation, which in the
Hinayâna aspect of Buddhism seems to be atheistic (all gods
of the popular religion are accepted, but they are only different forms of rebirth, of the wandering—and at the same time
in reality non-existing—soul!), this philosophy of salvation,
which wants to be agnostic and in which everyone is called
to be "his own Savior," receives sometimes a definitely mystical, religious tinge. By an apparent contradiction, Nirvâna
becomes then *the state of mystical approach* to the Unspoken,
Unutterable . . . Reality.

Here is a short survey of some designations of Nirvâna
that seemingly and sometimes definitely are patient not of
purely negative, but rather of positive sense: Nirvâna is
called the "Unutterable (*annakhata*), the "Unique" (*ke-
vala*), the "Infinite" (*ananta*), "Peace," "Security" (*yogak-
hema*), "State of Peaceful Rest" (*santapada*), "Blissful
Rest,"[31] "Health,"[32] "the Secure Foundation,"[33] "Absolute
Freedom,"[34] "the Unerring," "the True,"[35] "the Unchanging,"
"the Unperishing,"[36] "the Immortal" or "Not-Dying" (*amata*
—in Sanskrit: *amrta*),[37] or "the Immortal Region" (*amata*

[31]Dhammapad 368, 381; trans. by K. E. Neumann, *Die Reden Gotamo
Buddha's aus des Mittleren Sammlung,* vol. 1, p. 62 ff.
[32]Sutta Nipata 749.
[33]*Ibid.,* 946.
[34]Dhammapad 92.
[35]Sutta Nipata 758.
[36]*E.g.* Sutta Nipata 203, 1148, 1085; Dhammapad 225.
[37]*E.g.* Dhammapad 374; Mahavagga I, 5, 7; 5, 12; 23, 1; 23, 6; *Sacred
Books of the East,* vol. 13, pp. 86, 88, 144, 147. Cfr. Sutta Nipata 224.

dhatu),[38] "the Best," "the Highest" (*para* or *parama*), or "the Highest Good,"[39] "the Most Precious Jewel," "the Highest Bliss" (*paramam suttam*),[40] "the Immutable Bliss."[41] And suddenly out of the mouth of Buddha himself we hear the unexpected words: "There is, O monk, something Unborn that did not arise, that is uncreated, that has not sprung up. If, O monk, there were not this Unborn that did not arise, this Uncreated that has not sprung up, there would be no possibility of deliverance from that which is born, which did arise, which was created and which did spring up . . ."[42] It is as if a mystical strain, in flagrant contradiction with fundamental teachings of Hinayâna Buddhism (especially as they already took shape at the hands of early Buddhist theoreticians), was "smuggled" half unconsciously into the experience and the notion of Nirvâna.

Similar examples could be adduced in great number from the field of the history of religions. They show that theoretical belief does not cover nor does it limit all the possibilities of the contact of the soul with the Divine.

5.

Returning to the *duality* in the history of religions we can see, *e.g.,* the immense difference and the fundamental opposition between *prayer* and *magical practices* (notwithstanding that they often mingle together in the most indissoluble way). Magic is *coercion* of the higher power; it does not require piety of heart. Prayer may turn to magic if it is considered as having a force by itself, a coercive power over divinity. The cults of ancient Greece and the religions of India are full of magical elements—the rite by itself or the words by themselves have a power in them.

[38]Dhammapad 147.

[39]*E.g.* Sutta Nipata 627; cfr. 1086, *etc.*

[40]*E.g.* Dhammapadam 203, 204, 23; Sutta Nipata 268; cfr. Dhammapad 368-381.

[41]Udana VIII, 10. See my book *Zhazhda podlinnogo bytiya* (*Quest of the True Reality*, 1922), pp. 49-65.

[42]Udana VIII, 3; Itivuttaka 43.

And again there is duality—a most striking one—in the different phases through which *sacrifice* passed during the history of mankind, being a form of religious activity full of the deepest and also most complex significance.[43] It belongs to the center, to the core of religious experience and religious worship. It is a central element in the religious life of the Old Testament. The Christian message contemplates, with trembling admiration and thankful love, the supreme self-dedication of the Son of God: "And for their sake, I consecrate (dedicate—ἁγιάζω) Myself in order that they also might be consecrated by Truth." "I am the Good Shepherd. The Good Shepherd gives his life for the sake of the sheep." The immense condescending love of God fills up—through the voluntary act of total obedience and self-surrender unto death of the Son—the gap between the transcending and holy majesty of God and the fallen creature. The noblest acts of self-dedication of man, the yearning for a reconciliation with God through worship and sacrifice and humble obedience so strongly represented in the Old Testament (and outside the Old Testament) have here their redeeming and decisive and unique fulfilment. That is the Christian philosophy of history and philosophy of sacrifice. The obedience—unto death—of the Son that was made man is the point where the world is reconciled with God.[44]

But sacrifice is also the point, the sector of religious life most open to the possibility of an inroad of the forces of evil, as we can see from the history of sacrifice among different human races. We have only to think of the bloody human sacrifices to the Semitic Molochs[45] or of the absolutely horrifying sacrificial slaughter of human victims that had been practiced with greatest solemnity among the Aztecs of Mexico

[43]See for example the rich and probing chapter on sacrifice in Van der Leeuw, *Phaenomenologie der Religion* (1953), p. 327 ff.

[44]Cfr. Hebrews, Philip. 2, Rev. 5; or the teaching of Gregory of Nyssa or of Origen in his commentary on John 1:29; or the following passages from Origen's commentary on Leviticus: "More or less every sacrificial victim presents under some aspect the image of the Victim in which all others are recapitulated," Christ being "the perfect Victim of which all others are only a type and a figure" (Hom. 3, 5; Hom. 9, 8).

[45]See II(IV) Kings 23:10; Jer. 32:35.

to the honor of their gods Huitzilspochtli, Tezcalipoca and Tlaloc: 70,000 captives are reported to have been sacrificed in 1486 at the dedication of the great temple of Huitzilspolo-chtli.[46] The unscrupulous, cruel and hard-hearted Spanish *conquistadores* were simply horrified when they entered one of the buildings connected with the temple of Huitzilspolo-chtli and found it all full of human skulls and reeking and smelling with the bloody brains of the innumerable thousands of human victims spilled on the ground and the walls. The Spaniards received the definite impression that it was a worship of the Devil.

It is further sufficient to see the innumerable figures of demonic beings—half-men, half-animals with frightful tusks sticking out of their gaping jaws, with claws of snake-like tails ready to devour, figures that belong to the popular pantheon of India and crowd many Indian temples or are depicted in the famous Ajanta Caves[47] and that have their definite place in the people's worship—in order to realize that the holiest center of human activities and human energy—religion—could be corrupted by the breaking in of malign influences.

Corrupted in his holiest center of life, but not totally, and yearning—not always, but often enough—for goodness and mercy coming from above and listening for the distant call of the Divine, a call that is too often dimmed and distorted by our weakness and grossness and the inrush of the powers of evil—that is the picture of the history of man's religion contemplated from a Christian point of view.

6.

Evolution. Is there a regular evolution in the history of man's religion, a progress, a development, an ascension from

---

[46]See for example Prescott's *Conquest of Mexico*, vol. 1, ch. 3 (1922 ed. pp. 46-50); Fr. J. Clavigero, *Storia antigua del México* 6, 18 (Mexico City, 1943, vol. 2).

[47]*Paintings from the Ajanta Caves* (N.Y. Graphic Society and UNESCO), preface by J. Nehru.

lower to higher phases? I think that evolution can be *two-fold*: an ascending evolution and an evolution of decay, of deterioration. I think that both kinds of evolution have taken place in the history of man. But first a remark about the word evolution. If it means a mechanical, blind development, dictated only by the laws of nature (those also conceived as mechanical)—a concept that was wide-spread especially in the 19th and at the beginning of the 20th century—it would not be adequate to this complicated process, in which spiritual factors play a prominent, perhaps a decisive role: the freedom of man (be it only a partial freedom), his spiritual activity, and the Encounter.

From the Christian point of view there is a *plan of God* concerning the world, including the fact of man's free choice (although this freedom may be by and by utterly weakened) and the redeeming and restoring mercy of God. From this point of view there is, of course, a development, a movement onwards, but it can be as well ascending as descending because of the basic liberty of man, at any rate the liberty to fall or at least to yearn for ascension and salvation. And all that is included in the inscrutable redemptive plan of God, which is —alongside the freedom of the creature, man—the moving factor of the world's history and destiny. This point of view is very different from the purely "naturalistic" concept of evolution as it was theoretically developed in the 19th century, for example.

The concrete question that arises here before us is therefore the following: is there a regular and necessary ascension from lower forms to higher (parallel to the process which was considered as underlying the whole development of the realm of nature) in the history of human religion? That was the opinion of the philosopher Herbert Spencer, of Sir John Lubbock,[48] of Tylor (1832-1917) in his celebrated book *Primitive Culture* (1870) and many, many other scientists— be they anthropologists, ethnologists or historians of religion. This conception of a regular, thorough-going movement of ascension from the lower to the higher forms of religion does

[48]*The Origin of Civilization and the Primitive Condition of Man* (London, 1870).

not correspond to the historical, empirical data, as has been shown already by the great ethnologist and comparative historian of religion Andrew Lang in a series of books on the threshold between the 19th and the 20th centuries. He has clearly demonstrated two series of facts. First, that there is also another line of development traceable in the history of religion, a line which we may call *descending* evolution, an evolution from higher to lower forms, an evolution of distortion, of decay, of *deterioration*. This can be shown by the following examples. There are tribes, as, *e.g.,* the Pigmies of Central Africa and the natives of Southeast Australia, of Tierra del Fuego and of some islands of the Indian Ocean that in comparison with other primitive tribes, sometimes their neighbors, are on a much lower level of material civilization—in their technical achievements, *e.g.,* in the tools they use, and also in their social institutions. Therefore, from the point of view of the classical theory of evolution, they are more "primitive," more backward than the tribes possessing a more advanced technical civilization. At the same time the Pigmies of Central Africa possess a much higher religious conception of a Supreme God, Master of all beings and of the human destiny and author of a moral code, than most of their neighbors.[49] Similar things can be said of some Australian tribes. In the "Bora" or Australian mysteries, knowledge of "the Maker" and his commandments is imparted.[50] His precepts are: (1) To obey the old. (2) To share all with one's friends. (3) To live in peace with one's friends. (4) Not to interfere with girls or married women. (5) To obey the food restrictions. The supreme God of the Kurnai of Australia, who have very elaborated "mysteries," is called Mungun-Ngavr, "Our Father."[51] Of the god of the Andaman Islanders "Puluga" we are informed: he is "like fire," but invisible. He was never born and is immortal. By him were all things created, except the powers of evil. He knows even the thoughts

[49]See Paul Schebesta, "Die Religion der afrikanischen Pygmäen," in his *Christus und die Religionen der Erde* (1951), pp. 562-74.

[50]Andrew Lang, *The Making of Religion* (1898), p. 191.

[51]*Ibid.,* p. 196, quoting the great specialist on Australian tribes, Howitt, in the *Journal of the Anthropological Institute* (1885).

of the heart. He is angered by *yubda*—sin or wrong-doing—
that is, falsehood, theft, grave assault, murder, adultery, bad
carving of meat and (as a crime of witchcraft) burning of
wax. "To those in pain or distress he is pitiful and sometimes
deigns to afford relief." "He is Judge of Souls . . ."[52]

It seems that some of these and similar tribes have been
pushed back to the center of the big continent or to the wild
inhospitable islands by their more advanced and enterprising
neighbors. But this helped them to preserve their *higher
religious* faith that, as it seems in these cases, stood not at
the end, but at the beginning of the religious evolution which
in many cases seems to be an *evolution of descent, of religious
deterioration.* For these cases can be multiplied. To compile
and systematize the immense number of such data has been
the life-work of the great scholar—anthropologist, ethnologist
and historian of religion, editor of the review *Anthropos,*
professor of the universities of Vienna and Fribourg (in
Switzerland)—Fr. Wilhelm Schmidt (1868-1954), in his
gigantic work *Der Ursprung der Gottesidee* (*The Origin of
the Idea of God*) in 12 volumes (1912-1955). We need not
totally share the thesis of Pater Schmidt that a primordial
monotheistic conception can be *proved* in all cases as the
underlying base or rather starting point of all subsequent
religious developments. It is sufficient that Schmidt has shown
that the monotheistic conception is in many cases very old
among very primitive tribes and not necessarily the result of
a later development. On the contrary, there are definite signs
that in history of religion we have to reckon—at any rate in
many cases—with a primitive monotheistic belief, or a belief
approaching monotheism, and therefore with a strong line of
descending evolution (*i.e.,* of distortion and deterioration)
alongside other lines of *ascending* religious development (as, *e.g.,* in Greek philosophy from the beginnings to
Socrates and Plato or in the religious experience of the Old
Testament). From a Christian point of view this is easy to
understand: we have to reckon, as was said already, with

[52]*Ibid.*, p. 212, quoting Mann, who knows the language of the Andamanese
and has studied their religion, *Journal of the Anthropological Institute* 12,
p. 70.

human *freedom* (very weakened though it be through the fallen condition of man) and human *frailty* (*sin*) and with another and the most important factor, God, the Divine Reality that enters into contact with man and that can be apprehended by man, be it only in glimpses, by a very imperfect man, when he loses his better self and becomes submerged by floods of errors and gross superstitions. Here rises for a Christian the great fact of historical revelation, of *God's saving initiative,* of God's pedagogical and educative plan for man, of the possibility of the spiritual growth of man and of his progressive ascension to higher levels. It is not an impersonal mechanical evolution though: there is human freedom, the fact of a *quest* and the freedom of a *response* to God on the human side and the possibility of an encounter with the Divine and—more than that—of being laid hand upon by the loving and merciful God. This renders possible what we may call *leaps* in the field of moral and religious life, unexpected *creative changes* that are very different from a determinist evolution dictated by external unchangeable laws, as proclaimed by the older evolutionist theories.

Another example of a *descending* evolution in history of religion has been closely studied by the great Baltic German indologist (formerly professor of the University of Dorpat, later member of the Vienna Academy of Science) Leopold von Schroeder, in his book *Urarische Religion* (*Primitive Aryan Religion,* 1914).[53] By the analysis of the Rig-Veda hymns he comes to the conclusion that the dominant divinities of this collection—Indra (out of the 1028 hymns of the Rig-Veda 250 are dedicated to him), Agni (Fire, with 200 hymns) and Sôma (the personification of a holy beverage from the intoxicating juice of the plant *asclepias acida,* 114 hymns) —represent a lower religious conception and a *later* one (this can be proved by comparison with other Aryan religions) than the image of the heavenly god Varuna, Promoter and Keeper of Right (his name is related to the Greek Ouranos). Indra, the warlike and terrible giant whose forces are doubled

[53]Compare also the book on *Monotheistic Process in the Pagan World* (in Russian) by Prof. A. I. Vvedensky, of the Moscow Theological Academy, who about ten years before L. v. Schroeder comes to similar conclusions.

when he is intoxicated with the Sôma-juice (he himself is
boasting of it in a hymn) and who then smashes with his
club the skulls of the hostile demons, appealed more to the
Aryan conquerors who descended from the Pamir mountains
into the fertile valley of the Indus: he was more like themselves. So the conception of the King of Justice Varuna was
"pushed to the background" of their religion, but it was a
much higher conception! We can see this, *e.g.,* from the
following words addressed to Varuna:

> Sing forth a hymn, sublime and solemn, grateful to
>   glorious Varuna the imperial ruler,
> Who hath struck out, like one who slays the victim,
>   earth as a skin to spread in front of Surya . . . (Sun.)

> If we have sinned against the man who loves us, have
>   ever wronged a brother, friend, or comrade,
> The neighbor ever with us, or a stranger, O Varuna,
>   remove from us the trespass . . . (V 85)

In this case again the older conception of the Divinity was a
higher one.

But then there is again an ascending line in the history of
the religions of India. Both lines are closely interwoven in
the history of the so-called "pagan" religions, because, as
we have already seen, of the yearning of man for a higher
religious knowledge, but also . . . because of his weakness
and the fact that he easily capitulates before the surrounding
atmosphere of errors and superstitions and before the lower
passions of his own soul.

7.

There is something unique and unparalleled in the religious experience of the Old Testament that, in spite of many
points of contact with surrounding civilizations, makes it so
utterly different from all the religions of the ancient world.
What strikes us, even from a purely historical comparative

point of view, is *the permanence and the uninterrupted tradition* of its monotheistic faith, soaring to greater and greater heights in the religious experience of the spiritual leaders of Israel, leaders who too often have been persecuted by their own countrymen, but whose message, consigned to writing, becomes the holy books, the sacred treasure of the Jewish people. The unswerving monotheistic line, not in the life of wide circles of the people who during the period of kings were often only too eager to combine their allegiance to Jahve with the worship of alien, pagan gods, but in these leading prophetical personalities whose faith and religious experience at last prevailed and proved to be decisive—this line of monotheistic experience (that in many cases can be called an ascending line) strikes us with wonder and is simply unaccountable from purely evolutionary, historical presuppositions. It is an incomparable exception, standing forth—as we said—unequalled among the religions of the ancient world.[54] Even the pure and noble religion of Zoroaster cannot be compared with its intransigent, unflinching proclamation of the Only God, the Only Lord and Master. It is an historical enigma.

But if we approach this complex of unparalleled religious facts and experiences *from the inside, i.e.,* if we try to realize the very core, the deepest inner inspiration of this experience, we perceive some characteristic features that are even more striking.[55] We see that here the initiative *belongs to God*—not only in revealing Himself as Supreme and Holy and the One to Whom alone the plenitude of being belongs ("I am He Who Is!") and Who does not suffer and recognize any other deity beside Himself, but also as the One Who *supports* and *maintains* this true knowledge of Himself, in spite of the

[54]"If our records present Hebrew religion as something of an erratic boulder among the religions of the Near East, that is precisely what the subsequent developments demand": G. W. Anderson, "Hebrew Religion," in H. H. Rowley, *The Old Testament and Modern Study* (Oxford Pb., 1961), p. 300. Cfr. G. Ernest Wright, *The Old Testament Against its Environment* (London, SCM, 1950, repr. 1960).

[55]Thus Prof. Anderson speaks also of "the way in which the reader is taken, so to speak, inside the mind of the men of the Old Testament or enabled to see certain dominant and constant themes running through the entire development of the religion" (*loc. cit.*, p. 307).

faithlessness and inconstancies of the Jewish people. "I revealed Myself to those who did not ask for Me. I was found
by those who did not seek Me. I said: 'Here am I, here am I'
to a nation who did not call on My name. I spread My hands
all the day to rebellious people . . . a people that provoke
Me continually . . ." (Isaiah 65: 1-3). The initiative is God's:
He is spreading His arms to a rebellious people. He is meeting them more than half-way. He had elected them and He
is still condescending to them and drawing them to Himself,
by punishment for their unfaithfulness, by judgment and . . .
"bonds of compassion, bonds of mercy" (Hosea 11:5). So
His is the initiative: in revealing Himself to Abraham and
the patriarchs and to Moses and the prophets,[56] in revealing
His Holy Name to Moses, in the great act of salvation and
in the giving of the Law and concluding His covenant with
them, sending out the prophets,[57] even against their will,[58]
in punishment and help, in the destruction of their Holy City
and of His own temple—all that in order to move, to hit their
hardened, self-conceited heart—and in loving condescension
and pardon, announced by the prophets, along with the doom
and judgment. This is the leading, electing, chastising, destroying and . . . restoring, pardoning *initiative of God* trying
to awaken in their hearts a *response* to His faithfulness and
bounty, and to His severe and awe-inspiring holiness ("The
Lord your God is a devouring fire, a jealous God"—Deut.
4:24) and to His pardoning love ("See now that I, even I,
am He, and there is no God beside Me; I kill and I make
alive, I wound and I heal, and there is none that can deliver
out of My hand"—Deut. 32:39). And compare also these
words full of condescending love and majesty:

> And now, Israel, what does the Lord your God require
> of you, but to fear the Lord your God, to walk in all
> His ways, to love Him, to serve the Lord your God

[56]Walter Eichrodta calls this "der Tatcharakter der Gottesoffenbarung"
(in his *Theologie des Alten Testaments* [6th rev. edit., 1959], part 1, p. 10).

[57]See Isaiah 6.

[58]See Amos 7:15-16, Jer. 20:7-9. Compare the beautiful pages in L.
Bouyer, *La Bible et l'Evangile* (Paris, 1958), p. 19 ff.

with all your heart and all your soul, and to keep the commandments and the statutes of the Lord, which I command you this day for your good? Behold, to the Lord your God belong heaven and the heaven of heavens, the earth with all that is in it; yet the Lord set His heart in love upon your fathers and chose their descendants after them, you above all people . . . Circumcise therefore the foreskin of your heart, and be no longer stubborn. For the Lord our God is God of Gods and Lord of Lords, the Great, the Mighty and the Terrible God, Who is not partial and takes no bribes. He executes justice for the orphan and the widow, and loves the sojourner [the stranger] giving him food and clothing. (Deut. 10: 12-18).

This is the deepest sense of the progressive, pedagogical revelation of God in the Old Testament: to come to know God in His majesty and transcending, incomprehensible greatness and power and loving-kindness, and to fulfill His commandments and serve Him with a humble and loving heart, to trust in His pardon and His promise and to yearn for His Kingdom to come—a revelation that in the prophets (especially in Isaiah and Jeremiah) points to a new stage, beyond itself, to a new and more perfect covenant:

Behold, the days are coming, says the Lord, when I will make a new covenant with the house of Israel and the house of Judah, not like the covenant which I made with their fathers when I took them by the hand to bring them out of the land of Egypt, my covenant which they broke, though I was their husband, says the Lord. But this is the covenant which I will make with the house of Israel after those days, says the Lord, I will put my law *within them and I will write upon their hearts,* and I will be their God and they shall be my people . . . For I will forgive their iniquity and I will remember sin no more. (Jeremiah 31: 11-34)

But already in the experience and the revelation of the Old Testament what wonderful accents of yearning for God and of trust in Him, what deep feeling of His nearness and of His readiness to answer our prayer and stretch forth His helping hand into the abyss of our suffering!

As a hart longs for flowing streams, so longs my soul for Thee, O God!
My soul thirsts for God, for the living God.
When shall I come and behold the face of God? . . .
Why art thou cast down, O my soul, and why art thou troubled within me?
Hope in God, for I shall again praise Him, my salvation and my God. (Ps. 41 [42])

The Lord is my shepherd, I shall not want; he makes me lie down in green pastures.
He leads me beside still waters; He restores my soul.
He leads me in paths of righteousness, for His Name's sake.
Even though I walk through the valley of the shadow of death,
I fear no evil: for Thou art with me: Thy rod and Thy staff, they comfort me . . . (Ps. 22 [23]: 1-4)

These accents of fervent supplication, this lifting up of the heart towards God, this crying out to God from the depth of the abyss, this trust and confidence, the impassionate stretching of the soul towards God, its sole Refuge and Helper, and this rejoicing in the Lord are incomparable. They have been adopted by the Christian Church as the best expression of this turning of the soul towards her God in distress and anguish and in thankful praise.

Whom have I in heaven but Thee? And there is nothing on earth that I desire but Thee.
My flesh and my heart are failing. But God is the strength of my heart and my part for ever. (Ps. 72 [73]:25-26)

The overwhelming omnipresence of God, *i.e.,* His near-ness to me wherever I am, His greatness and incomprehensi-bility and saving Presence, and the support of His mighty and merciful arm are depicted in Psalm 138 (139):

O Lord, Thou hast searched me and known me!

Thou knowest when I sit down and when I rise up; Thou discernest my thoughts from afar . . .

Even before a word is on my tongue, lo, O Lord, Thou knowest it perfectly.

Thou dost beset me behind and before, and layest Thy hand upon me . . .

Whither shall I go from Thy Spirit? Or whither shall I flee from Thy presence?

If I ascend to heaven, Thou art there! If I make my bed in Sheol, Thou art there!

If I take the wings of the morning and dwell in the uttermost parts of the sea,

Even there Thy hand shall lead me, and Thy right hand shall support me . . . (Ps. 138 [139]: 1,2,4,5, 7-10)

One of the highest expressions of this piety of the Old Testament we find in the longest and perhaps one of the most beautiful psalms—Psalm 118 (119). It describes the delight of the soul in the Word of God, in His command-ments; and it is a fervent prayer, ascending to Him from the depth, a fervent hope and a cry for salvation.

Blessed are those who keep His testimonies, who seek Him with their whole heart . . .

Thou hast commanded Thy precept to be kept diligently.

O that my ways may be steadfast in keeping Thy statutes . . .

I will observe Thy statutes; O forsake me not utterly . . .

With my whole heart I seek Thee; let me not wander from Thy commandments . . .

Thy testimonies are wonderful, therefore my soul keeps them . . .

I open my mouth and I sigh, because I long for Thy commandments.

Turn to me and be gracious to me as is Thy wont towards those who love Thy name. . . .

With my whole heart I cry; answer me, O Lord. I will keep Thy statutes.

I cry to Thee; save me, and I may observe Thy testimonies . . .

Look on my affliction and deliver me, for I do not forget Thy law . . .

Let my cry come before Thee, O Lord; give me understanding according to Thy word!

Let my supplication come before Thee; deliver me according to Thy word . . .

Let Thy hand be ready to help me, for I have chosen Thy precepts.

I long for Thy salvation, O Lord, and Thy law is my delight . . .

I have gone astray like a lost sheep; seek Thy servant: for I have not forgotten Thy commandments. (Ps. 118 [119]: 2, 4, 5, 8, 10, 129, 131, 132, 145, 146, 169, 170, 173, 174, 176)

The highest revelation of the Old Testament, pointing beyond itself, is that of the coming Righteous One, Who will take upon Himself our sins, our diseases and our suffering.

He is despised and rejected by men, a man of sorrow and acquainted with grief . . . But He has borne our griefs and carried our sorrows . . . He was wounded for our transgressions . . . upon Him was the chastisement that made us whole, and with His stripes we are healed. All we like sheep have gone astray . . . and the Lord has laid on Him the iniquity of us all. He was oppressed and He was afflicted, yet He opened not

His mouth. Like a lamb that is led to the slaughter and like a sheep that before its shearer is dumb, so He opened not His mouth . . . although He had done no violence and there was no deceit in His mouth . . . Yet he bore the sin of many and made intercession for the transgressors. (Isaiah 53)

The New Testament speaks of the *fulfilment*: it *has been achieved*. The reconciliation has taken place, the abyss is filled up by the condescension of Him who became our Brother. ("It is consummated"—John 19:30.)

4

Plato's Religious Message

This is one of the highest summits—or definitely the highest—of Greek religious thought.

It did not arise abruptly. It was prepared: by Parmenides, by Heraclitus and then, in the first place, by the extraordinary personality and the deep moral and—let us venture the word—mystical experience of Socrates. And yet it is a *jump*, a being uplifted in a new dimension, a sudden revelation of *another*, a higher Reality. That which was dimly felt and hinted at by the great Heraclitus,[1] that which inspired the pedagogical-prophetical work of Socrates, was now explicitly stated and contemplated by the spiritual eye: the real Reality, that which is the home and goal and object of aspiration of the soul, the *real world* of unpolluted Beauty, the immense ocean of primordial Beauty (τὸ πολὺ πέλαγος τοῦ καλοῦ),[2] unalloyed, uncontaminated by mortal dust, the Beauty that is eternal, not subject either to becoming or to extinction, that neither grows nor decays, that is not beautiful from one point of view and ugly from another . . . but herself the Divine Beauty, in her simplicity and unity.[3] To preach, to proclaim the *real Reality* (τὸ ὄντος ὄν),[4] as opposed to our deceitful and shadowy world, as the light of the real Sun is opposed to the illusory images (which are only shadows of shadows, reflection of reflections seen by the poor prisoners of the dark

---

[1]Τὸ σοφόν ἐστὶ τὸ τῶν πάντων κεχωρισμένον—"The Wise (*i.e.*, the true Divine Reality of the Logos) is that which is separated from all things."
[2]*Sympos.* 210 D.
[3]*Sympos.* 210 E - 211 E.
[4]*Phaed.* 24, I C.

cave and considered by them to be the only reality: see
Republic, book VII): this proclaiming, this opposition, this
inspired witness to the real Reality and the call to lift up the
mind's eye toward it—this is the ultimate purport, the soul of
Plato's philosophy (which is very rich and complex, com-
prising many different elements and problems). But that is
the chief problem among all, the main purpose: to escape from
the darkness of the cave and to lift up one's eye to the rays
of the Sun Eternal. And Plato is full of such appeals, of
such teachings, of such nostalgia. For there is the true harbor
of the soul, the source and goal of her yearning, of her "hunt
after that which really is."[5] "To one who arrives there it is
like a rest from his travelling and the end of his journey."[6]
The "flight" thither is "assimilation to God as far as possible";[7] during his lifetime the soul of the wise, fleeing the
sensual and following Reason, "contemplates the True, the
Divine and Immutable and is nourished thereby."[8]

And above all other ideas rises and reigns the idea of the
Good. It is higher than the knowledge and being, says Plato.[9]
But it is difficult to contemplate (μόγις ὁρᾶται),[10] so great
is its perfection. This is the platonic conception of the Supreme
Divine Being. Of course, it is impersonal, it is not a living
and loving God, but it inspires the soul with immense desire.
It is the goal and center that gives sense to life, it proves also
to be the inspiring center of Plato's religious philosophy.

The discovery of Another—of the primordial, the only
really Real, of Spiritual Reality, of the *Divine as utterly
different from the world*—that is the great feat of Plato's
philosophy. A source of new spiritual insight entered through
him into the ancient world. Of Plato's philosophy we can
with special reason use the words dear to many apologists:
praeparatio evangelica. It proclaims the Divine Reality and

[5]*Phaed.* 66 C: τὴν τοῦ ὄντος θήραν.
[6]*Rep.* VII, 532 E.
[7]*Theaet.* 176 B.
[8]*Phaed.* 84 A.
[9]*Rep.* VI, 509 B: ". . . not only knowledge proceeds from the Good, but
also being and essence, the Good itself being not essence, but by far exceed-
ing it."
[10]*Rep.* VII, 517 C.

shows at the same time the abyss between it and us. And this sense of an abyss separating the two worlds forms one of the chiefest and most central problems of Plato's philosophy. This makes it so full of tension, yea, even of dramatic tension.

There is a *duality* in Plato's approach to this our world, this cosmos, and to its relation to the upper world of immutable, immortal ideas. Sometimes this our world is considered a true reflection of the higher one, and then it is spoken of in tones of highest praise and admiration. So in the *Timaeus* our world is even called "a second god" (δεύτερος θεὸς) and to vilify it is said to be something unsuitable, unlawful, impious (οὐ θέμις ἐστίν). Here the Hellenic strain in the mind of Plato, the Hellenic inheritance is felt very strongly. He loves and admires the harmony and balance and beauty of the cosmos, as we have seen it already in the philosophy of Heraclitus, as we shall meet it later in the philosophy of the Stoics, but also in later Platonists, Neopythagoreans and Neoplatonists. This sense of harmony and balanced order and beauty in the world is a basic and deeply-rooted part of the Greek outlook.

And the love of beauty, of earthly beauty that permeates his pages, the charming setting of his dialogues, the charming forwardness of his Athenian boys, who make Socrates "prisoner" (so in the *Republic*) until he answers all their questions and thus enter into the most arduous and difficult discussions of the sense of human affairs and human life, the playful vividness of the dialogues, the atmosphere of earnestness and radicalism in the search of truth and of youthful grace that is exhaled by those boys of Athens—all this shows how deeply Plato is rooted in the brilliant world of Greek culture and how he delights therein.

But on the other hand Plato feels this world and its way of life as deceitful, unreal and full of wickedness, fundamentally opposed in its mutability, instability and injustice to the world of Divine Immutable Truth. It is sufficient to read the description of the true philosopher in his *Theaetetus*: he has "never from his youth known his way to the people's meetingplace, he does not know where the court is or the

council or any political assembly, he lives in the city only
with his body, but his mind is inquiring into the nature of
things."[11] Plato was one of those most struck and wounded
by the great moral tragedy of Athens: the condemnation to
death "by the regular Athenian people's court in regular proceeding" of his beloved teacher, the just among the just, the
seeker and proclaimer of Truth—Socrates. The leading Greek
city, the greatest center of Greek culture, condemned to death
the man of whom this city ought to have been proud, its
faithful and greatest son, its leader on the way to virtue and
truth, the man who untiringly endeavored to awaken in its
citizens the sense of moral duty and moral responsibility.
After that, what was human justice worth? The court of the
noblest city in Greece condemned to death its noblest son.
After that, it becomes clear that no real justice is to be ex-
pected on earth. After that, the highest civic and democratic
slogans and institutions are only a lie and a deceit. Therefore
there is no place here on earth, in those earthly states and
cities, in those institutions, democracies, or tyrannies or
monarchies, for a seeker of Truth. And moreover all things
pass, are in perpetual flow. Plato was well aware of this,
having also listened to a disciple of Heraclitus—Cratylus. And
what worth are things that pass? The wise man is in quest
of those things *that remain for ever.*

   This *dualism* of Plato's outlook is one of the most important and—we can say—dramatic features in the development
of his thought.[12] On the one hand, true Reality belongs only
to the eternal and immutable realm of the ideas, the divine
prototypes and sources of all that is. On the other hand, this
world of ours is palpable enough; and although it possesses
only a shadowy existence, which cannot even be apprehended
by regular thinking but only by a sort of "unlawful" one
(νόθοι λογισμοί), this shadowy world, not even existing in
the true sense of the word, is powerful enough to block, to

[11]*Theaet.* 173-174; *Gorgias* 526.

[12]See about it, for example, the essay of Vladimir Soloviev, *Zhizhnenaya
drama Platona (The Tragedy of Plato)*; Prince E. Trubetzkoy, *Sozialnaya
utopia Platona* (1908); R. Eucken, *Die Lebensanschauung der grossen
Denker;* Entz, *Pessimismus und Weltflucht bei Plato* (1911).

obscure, to distort, to render ineffective the power of Divine Reality. What then remains to us? Only *flight* to the real, the higher world; as soon as possible, the flight "from here thither."[13]

There is a rupture, a contradiction in the thought of Plato—the passionate interest in this world and the proclamation of its harmony and beauty, and the total rejection of this world as totally insufficient, deceiving and vain, as hopelessly, un-redeemingly subject to evil and corruption—a rupture, a contradiction that makes his thought so much deeper and richer and so full of developments and of dramatic tensions, and that is so often present at the back of his mind. And then arises the desire to overcome this essential, inner opposition of the two worlds—the real one and ours, the shadowy one—*to throw a bridge over this abyss between these two worlds.* Much of Plato's philosophical endeavor is dedicated to the problem of *building a bridge* between the two worlds.

There is a rupture, a contradiction in the thought of Plato—between the transcendent world of the pure ideas and our mortal, deceitful "reality": his doctrine of *eros* (the yearning of love) as the ladder that raises us from earthly objects of love to divine primordial Beauty (in his *Symposium*); and the dreams and more than dreams—a detailed scheme—of a *perfect state,* as visualized by him especially in his famous *Republic.* Both bridges proved to be ineffective. Eros remains a mainly *subjective* ladder: we are climbing upon it from our rapturous love for a single human body to the love of all bodily beauty and then higher—to the love for all beautiful things of the mind, of the spiritual order, until we have reached the ocean of primordial Beauty, untainted by mortal dust, by earthly forms and figures, not passing and waning away, not beautiful in one aspect but lacking beauty from another point of view, but *Beauty Itself,* pure and immutable

[13]*Theaet.* 176 A: "Evil can never pass away; for there must always re-main something that is opposed to Good. As there is no place for it among the gods in heaven, it must of necessity dwell around the mortal nature, in this earthly sphere. Therefore we must *fly* from here *thither* as soon as possible."

and immortal. Should not the soul contemplating that forever
be considered as blissful?

This is (along with the vision of the Supreme Realities in
Phaedrus) one of the most inspired passages in Plato. The
soul has climbed to the top of the ladder of eros and has
immersed itself in the pure ocean of Beauty Celestial. But the
ladder itself, its lower rungs upon which we climbed to the
top, *remain unredeemed*, are simply transcended and left
behind. It is a subjective crossing over the abyss. The abyss
remains gaping, it is not filled up by the power of Redeeming
Love, transfiguring the earthly and mortal.

And the ideal state of Plato's *Republic* proves to be not
ideal at all; it is not at all the kingdom of Divine Reality on
earth, the transfiguration of an earthly republic into a Divine
City.

We cannot read certain passages of Plato's *Republic* without feeling the deep emotion that permeates it. It is like
strokes of wings, following one after another, that bear us
into higher regions. There is an immense spiritual beauty and
nostalgia in the words of Plato concerning those "who are
lovers of the vision of Truth," those "who see the Absolute
and Eternal and Immutable"—the philosophers "holding con-
verse with the Divine Order." According to Plato only those
who "have the perfect vision of the Other World" are called
"to order laws about beauty, goodness, justice in this world,
and to guard and preserve the order of them."[14] Only true
philosophers have to rule the ideal state.

But there is so much that is unconvincing, strange and
even naive in this picture of Plato's. It is not the Kingdom of
God on earth. It is a mixture of communism, denying some
unalienable human rights—the right to have one's own family,
the right of the parents to their children (for the two higher
ruling classes)—, with a *static* conception of his utopia. There
is no further development inside his scheme once it is attained.
It is like a pyramid: only those who are on top, the philosophers, are called to the knowledge of Eternal Truth. The
lower, working classes remain in their false conventional

[14]*Rep.* V, 475, 979, VI, 500, 484 (I quote here Jowett's translation); compare also R. L. Nettleship, *Lectures on the Republic of Plato.*

opinions and continue their usual lives under the wise guidance and supervision of the intermediate class—the guardians
and warriors. The participation in the true life of the Spirit is
open only to the few. And even those few—the philosophers
—have to be dragged down, compelled to descend among their
fellow-citizens to take care of the affairs of the state.[15] It is
not only a baffling mixture of mystic inspiration with abstract
planning; this scheme of a state is constructed on the denial
of human freedom and some most elementary and fundamental rights of human personality. And there is no uplifting
of the Whole in a higher sphere, no hope of an ultimate
transfiguration. It is neither the kingdom of perfect justice on
earth nor the bridge to be thrown over the abyss separating
the two worlds.

Plato has preached deliverance—for the lonely wise man
whose life is "a preparation to death" (μελέτη θανάτου)[16]
and a nostalgia for the Supreme Reality, a yearning, a stretching forth toward it. Salvation is in the spiritual flight "from
here thither." But the world remains unchangeable—in its
beauty and its becoming doomed to permanent death and
permanent passing away and to the presence of evil. "The
Evil cannot be abolished because there always must be something opposed to the Good. But it cannot dwell with the
gods in heaven. So it has to dwell here among us in our
sphere. Therefore we must *flee* from here *thither* as soon as
possible."[17] That is the last word of Plato's religious and
mystical experience. But the world remains unrelieved. The
unchangeable status of this world of ours, the power of
inertia, death and corruption inseparable from matter, proved
to be stronger than the power of the abstract philosophical
god of Plato—not the Personal Living God, Creator and
Redeemer—and the world in its totality has to remain unredeemed.

The successors of Plato, especially during the whole last,
predominantly religious period of Greek philosophy, have
inherited this problem: the abyss between the world of Divine

[15]*Rep.* VII, 59.
[16]*Phaed.* 81 A.
[17]*Theaet.* 176 A. See above.

Reality and this world of ours, and the yearning, the desire to fill up the gap. But it could not be achieved by way of philosophy.

The Christian Gospel proclaimed the *breaking through of the Divine Reality* into this world and the filling up of the chasm by the coming in flesh, by the death and resurrection of the Son of God.

5

The Mystical Encounter

1.

There are some preliminary questions about mystical experience, some weighty objections to handle. Is there not a strain of unnatural hysterical emotionalism in the so-called mystical experience, a self-indulgence in highstrung, exuberant, strange, if not abnormal, feelings and often even a self-induced, intentional, thus unnatural and artificial, fostering of such exceptional states of mind? This is true in many cases, but the fact that there are artificially produced, intentionally self-provoked states of mind does not exclude that there might also be genuine and spontaneous ones. But in general are those mystical states of mind healthy and acceptable from a moral or religious point of view, even if they are spontaneous and genuine? Is this not an inrush of tumultuous waves of suppressed passions and emotions streaming forth from our sub-consciousness into our conscious mind, a morbid emotionalism submerging the sense of responsibility, which is so important in religious and moral life, that sober and humble standing before the face of God, united to moral endeavor and moral struggle which is basic for the Christian attitude? We must make here a quite definite distinction between *pantheistic* and *theistic* mysticism, the first being by its very character—immersion into the great impersonal life of the universe by suppressing any conscious moral personality—especially subject to such tendencies. But on the other hand we see that there are many great mystics—especially among Christian saints—who are full of a deep sense of moral responsibility. There are the great mystics of the Christian East who feel strong misgivings and distrust as to all sorts of religious emotionalism and who sternly and decisively reject all kinds of disorderly exuberance of feeling, all kinds of spiritual "greediness," all immature pursuits of spiritual sensations as dangerous and often misleading (see especially the writings of Gregory of Sinai, 14th century). And herein they are also backed by some of the greatest among the mystical teachers of the Christian West—in first place by John of the Cross and Theresa of Spain. This emotional, unbalanced and unbridled exuberance is indeed often met in mysticism and mystical writers, especially of the pantheistic sort, but it must be considered as an aberration, a falling away from the true mystical line, as a yielding to the temptations of human emotional self-indulgence even in this holy field of religious experience. It means that this objection is valid in regard to many phenomena representing aberrations of the mystical life, but not to the mystical life and mystical experience as such. And it is also not true that mystical experience makes man unsuited for the requirements and responsibilities of practical life, for the fulfillment of moral obligations, for the service of the brethren. Many great Christian mystics were also persons of a burning, heroic, self-forgetting love for the fellow-men and of immense achievements, even in the field of practical, social life. Let us think of the great founders of monasteries and monastic congregations in the East and in the West, some of whom were also great mystics, for example Francis of Assisi, Teresa de Jesus, Symeon the New Theologian, Abbot Paisius Velichkovsky (1722-1794) and many others.

But the last and perhaps the weightiest of all objections still remains. Let us admit that there is a genuine mysticism, which is not purely emotional self-indulgence, and that some of the greatest heroes of religious life and of the life of loving self-dedication to God and the fellow-men have been mystics; moreover, let us admit that their mystical experience was that which inspired them to their heroic deeds of love and self-dedication, that those great mystics belong to the

highest summits of spiritual life attained by us. But what
does it mean? Are those not *exceptional* cases? What have
they to do with *our* lives, with *our* case, with our goal, our
achievements, our struggle? Is it not something which belongs
to quite another level, truly inspiring reverence, but hopelessly
distant from us, bearing no resemblance to our experience
and therefore having no practical bearing or presenting no
practical applications for us? Is it not just a case to study
from a psychological or scholarly point of view (most interesting as what in German is called *Grenzfall*: a case on the
utmost margin of the experience), or to revere as an exceptional achievement of a few great and lonely individuals, far
away from us and very unlike us? Let us study mysticism
as an interesting chapter of comparative history of religion,
but let us admit that it is something, as it were, exotic, concerning us very little.

This point of view sounds very plausible, but it is utterly
false; just the contrary is true. Genuine mystical experience
—let it be vouchedsafe only to a few individuals—is something
of immense importance, of *central and decisive importance*
for us all. It concerns us in a most direct and most stringent
way. The mystics are pioneers of our race. They were con-
cerned—in an exceptionally all-engrossing way—with what
we are living from, with the central, the only really important
Reality: with the Reality of God. They proclaim this all-
decisive, this all-conditioning, this overwhelming Reality of
God, being themselves captured and overwhelmed and subjected thereby. From immediate experience the mystics come
to know that which is of utmost concern for us all. There are
moments that decide their whole life. The soul is confronted
with the Reality of God, with the Presence of Him who is
Life Eternal. It is laid hand upon, it is captured thereby,
often for life. So was it with Paul. Not he, but the Lord
becomes the innermost inspiration and creative center of his
life. Not he lives forthwith, but Christ lives in him. He is
only the unworthy servant: "Paul—the slave of Jesus Christ."
"αἰχμαλωθήσεται"—the soul is "made prisoner" of things
sublime and unutterable, says Macarius of Egypt. The subjugating, transcending Reality is here, present and quite near.

It has dawned on my sight, and my eyes have suddenly been opened. I have touched the skirts of His garment, and He has taken hold of me. I bow before Him, and I fall to the ground before His immense majesty, power and glory. I kneel before Him and adore Him.

There are always two sides, two aspects in authentic mystical experience: the vision of the majesty and glory of God, and of my own misery, nakedness and smallness. This is especially characteristic and basic in a theistic attitude, and it is of primary importance for Christian mystical experience. "Who am I, Thy unworthy slave and the little worm before Thee?" said Francis of Assisi. "I cry and sob when I see the all-transcending light and my own nakedness," says the Byzantine mystic of the 11th century, Symeon the New Theologian. I am nought, just dust and ashes, and I own nothing. Now I know it, now at last I see it: because He has deigned to approach me, to reveal Himself to me. He in His mercy has condescended to stoop down to me. He is there, He knocks at the door, He wants me to let Him in. "My Lord, I am unworthy that Thou shouldest enter under the roof of my house: for it is all in ruins. But do enter! Say a word, and my soul will be healed": this is the trend of the prayers before participation in the Lord's Supper, in the Christian East and West.

He is here, and I am falling on my face before Him. And I am dedicating all my life to Him. He has taken it, but I agree joyfully to it. There is bliss and certainty in this utter self-surrender. It is a burning away of all unworthy, selfish regards, of all scales, all rubbish, and uncleanness of the soul. For He is devouring fire. "O lámparas de fuego!" exclaims John of the Cross ("O flashes of fire!"). Pascal writes on the very night of his conversion: "From 11:30 in the evening till 1:50 at night—Fire!—God of Abraham, Isaac and Jacob, and not of the philosophers and the wise." Here at last he finds: "Certainty, certainty . . . joy, peace!" And the soul overwhelmed sheds tears of joy and thankfulness before her God ("Joie, joie, pleurs de joie!"). The soul has found the peace of God, it means that now she is rooted; she knows to Whom she belongs, and that in Him is peace.

Then there begins a transvaluation of all values. All that shortly before seemed precious and important has lost its worth. It is dust and nothing. Paul decided to count all things and all the privileges of birth, of education, of righteousness according to the law as dung in order to acquire Christ. Plotinus says that the soul discards and rejects all that she before valued in order to acquire that which transcends all and which alone is important. "We have nothing and we possess all," writes Paul to the Corinthians. "I have lost the flock that I guarded before," says the soul in the mystical poem of John of the Cross ("Y el ganada perdi que antes seguia").

There is a new life, a "newness of life" kindled in man, but a *living life,* a free and creative process on the lines of *personality,* not a mechanical repercussion. That brings us to the other side of mystical experience: the response of man to the initiative of God.

2.

Knocking at the door of the heart is not sufficient, knocking does not help, if—to emphasize it once more—the heart does not open its door. And when it is opened, the Lord enters and takes abode in the heart. This is the deepest significance of the Christian eucharistic experience and of the mystical life in general. His entering my heart and reigning therein is the highest goal of the new life. The soul must therefore prepare itself, it must see its own unworthiness and nakedness, it must humble itself, it must try to clean itself and surrender itself to the Lord. "I have surrendered all the keys of my house to Divine Love," says Catherine of Genoa. In meekness and humility I surrender through a manly, courageous struggle with my old self. That is the meaning of Christian co-crucifixion with the Lord. Only in manfully sharing His self-surrender, obedience unto death and suffering can I come to share His Life.

Self-surrender of our will to God is the highest achievement on the way leading us from man to God. We find this expressed in many utterances of great mystics representing the *theistic* religious experience, *i.e.*, the encounter of two living personalities: the Divine and the human. We also find such utterances outside of Christianity, in the mystical confessions of some medieval theistic mystics of India or among the Sufis, with their blending of two strains, the theistic and the pantheistic.

Bayezid Bestami, the great Sufi of the 9th century, hears the voice of God speaking to his soul in the night: "What dost thou desire, Bayezid?—That which Thou desirest, O my God!—O Bayezid, I desire thee, as thou desirest Me.—But what way leads to Thee?—O Bayezid, the man that renounces himself, he comes to Me." And Bayezid, feeling himself aflame with boundless love, exclaims, "O my God, I desire from Thee only Thee. Take away from my heart all that is not Thee."[1]

And now to quote some of the Indian saints and mystics: "Dispose according to Thy will with me Thy slave, Thy property. For Tulasai belongs to Thee alone. I am only a sacrificial gift, thrown under Thy feet," says Tulasai-Dasa (a poet of the 16th century) in a hymn.[2] "Whatsoever I am in soul and body and whatsoever qualities I own," exclaims another poet and mystic Yamuna-Muni, "all this I gather in one heap and throw at Thy feet, O Lord. All that is mine and what I am myself must belong to Thee."[3] "Thy slave offers himself to Thee with a free heart," sings Nanak.[4]

The difference from the Christian experience consists in the fact that the surrendering of one's will to God, the supreme act of obedience, the return of many to the unity with God is something unattainable for man by his own effort, according to the Christian conviction. Man cannot achieve it; it has been achieved once: in the supreme sacrifice of His will offered by the Only-Begotten Son to His Father. And we share in His sacrifice, we are uplifted by His offering.

[1]Tezkireh-i-Evlia, *Le memorial des saints*, trans. by A. Pavet de Courteville (Paris, 1883), pp. 127, 131, 132.

[2]Quoted by Fr. Heiler in his book *Das Gebet* (1978), p. 250.

[3]Otto Vishnu-Narayana, *Texte zur indischen Gottesmystik*, vol. 1 (1917), p. 50.

[4]Heiler, *op. cit.*

We are obedient *only* through His sacrifice, only through His obedience. For Christians and for Christian mysticism Christ is not only the supreme guide to God: He is God Himself, having come to us and dwelt among us and having really become man and as man having really offered His will and His life in sacrifice of obedience to His Heavenly Father, making us share His obedience, His suffering, His cross, and through it—only through it—His Life Eternal. The Christian fact, the Christian Good Tidings, is *mystical and historical reality*: here, in the flesh, among us in the fulness of the Godhead. Through Him and with Him, our Lord and our Brother, we return to union with God. "Abide in Me and I will abide in you." "Not I live henceforth; Christ lives in me."

6

Characteristic Features of the Christian Message

What are the characteristic features of Christianity? The innermost center and the whole substance of the Christian Good Tidings is the boundless *condescension of God,* the inrush of God into the world, the concrete, historical, supreme and unique revelation of God's infinite love, the Son of God having descended to become one of us and ascended, thus enabling us to ascend with Him.

We have spoken already of the sense of a subjugating, overpowering Presence, or Reality, transcending all and, at the same time, so near and taking hold of us, as the basic feature of mystical experience. Now, if we compare this with the experience of primitive Christianity, what do we see? We find in the primitive Christian experience the same sense of a mystical Presence, *but* connected with a *definite historical* Person, manifested in the flesh. Something, or rather Somebody, quite concrete, definite, unique, historical, "that which we have seen with our eyes and which we have gazed upon and *our hands have handled"*—and this was the Word of Life, the Life Eternal (I John 1:1-2).

The whole Gospel narrative, meaning the whole primitive preaching, is permeated by this sense of a transcending, overpowering Presence. This keynote is struck at once in the opening words of the Gospel according to Mark: "The beginning of the Gospel of Jesus Christ, Son of God. As it has been written by Isaiah the prophet: Lo, I send my messenger before Thy face, which shall prepare Thy way before Thee.

The voice of one crying in the wilderness, Prepare ye the way of the Lord, make His paths straight!" John, the great prophet, appears then on the scene, but he speaks of the coming of One infinitely greater than he, for he, John, is unworthy to stoop down and to unloose the latches of His shoes! This key-note dominates and permeates all that follows. The first chapter of Mark reproduces the happenings crowded into one eventful day on the shores of the lake of Galilee. He addresses His call to simple fishermen, and they leave all and follow Him. He heals "many that were sick of diverse diseases" and casts out demons. The faith kindled by Him is so great that a roof is opened in order that a paralytic might be lowered down on his bed to where Jesus was. This sense of a transcending Presence permeates all of the other Gospels as well. Remember how Peter, in the story of the miraculous fishing (Luke 5), is overcome by a sense of awe. He feels that he is in the presence of Someone who transcends the limits of the purely human: "Depart from me, for I am a sinful man, O Lord!" One could say that the binding thread running through all the narratives of Luke's gospel, especially from chapter 4 to chapter 12, is the awareness of an overpowering Presence, introduced by the scene in the synagogue of Nazareth, where Jesus applies to Himself the words of the prophecy of Isaiah: "The Spirit of the Lord is upon Me, therefore He has anointed Me . . ." "And all bore witness and wondered at the words of grace proceeding from His mouth."

The idea prominent in the whole of the apostolic preaching is *fulfillment*. "This day this scripture is fulfilled in your ears." The promises of God are being fulfilled *now*, here, before our eyes. The central event in the history of the world is taking place. Kings and prophets have yearned—vainly—to see and hear that which now is revealed to the eyes and ears of the disciples. *Here* and *now* is the Center, the Refuge, the place of Rest, the place of Reunion with God, the entrance to the Kingdom. "Lo, the Kingdom of Heaven is among you." "Come unto Me all you that travail and are heavy laden." The Gospel narratives—especially in Luke—often describe the encounter between a repentant sinner and the merciful Lord—for example the stories of Zacchaeus, of the good thief, the repenting woman who poured precious balm on Christ's feet, the publican and the pharisee. The idea and the experience of the mystical encounter with one's Savior, so central and decisive for Christian devotional life throughout the centuries, is deeply rooted in the New Testamental experience in its most decisive, most primitive and fundamental strata.

But, as we have seen, it is more than that. The decisive center of history has been attained and revealed, the fulness of times has come. All that had come before was a preparation; now is the plenitude, the fulfillment, the consummation. "It is consummated!" (not "finished," as it is rendered in the King James' version—τετέλεσται, John 19:30).

We understand why the idea of *witness*—or rather the fact of being a witness—is so characteristic of the apostolic preaching. The preaching is not a proclamation of abstract ideas or, in the first place, moral precepts. It is something different, something most striking, and peculiar—it is the proclamation of that which they "have seen with their eyes and heard with their ears and what their hands had handled." They are speaking of *facts* belonging to the texture of *history*, to the texture of this their life, their surroundings. They have been with Him, they have talked with Him, they have touched Him with their hands, they have eaten with Him, even "after His resurrection from the dead" (Acts 10:41). This is most concrete, most definite and palpable, but it is not all. Witness-bearing means more than that. It includes simultaneously two planes, two realities, or rather *one* Reality given simultaneously in its two real aspects: the *Word of God* that really *became Flesh*. This is the Johannine vision ("we have seen . . . His glory"): divine Reality and Flesh which the Word became, bound together in a most intimate, indissoluble way; and the witness is a contemplation and proclamation of these two realities which are but *one*—in the Son of God, who took abode among us and whose glory we have contemplated. This "Johannine" standpoint is the real presupposition of the whole preaching; it is the substance of this witness, of Christianity.

Fact—historical, concrete, circumscribed by time and environment—and divine Reality—the unique inrush, the break-
ing-through of God into the history of man, His Presence
among us in flesh and factual history: on this fact, historical
and mystical, on this divine concreteness and historicity, the
whole salvation is founded. Without this historical fact, there
is no salvation. Paul, after having spoken in I Corinthians of
the gifts of the Spirit, and the heights of the spiritual life,
suddenly returns with all his emphasis to simple historical
fact. As in chapter 2 he had already written: "I determined
not to know anything among you, save Jesus Christ and Him
crucified," so now he makes this celebrated profession of
faith which is the first Christian *symbolum fidei*: "Now, I
declare unto you, brethren, the gospel which I preached unto
you, which also ye have received and wherein also you stand;
by which also ye are saved, if ye hold fast that which I
preached unto you, unless ye have believed in vain. For I
delivered unto you first of all that which I also received, how
Christ died for our sins according to the Scriptures; and that
He was buried, and that He rose again the third day according to the Scriptures and that He appeared to Cephas, then
to the Twelve . . ." That is the basis of faith, that is whereon
salvation depends: His death and His resurrection. "If Christ
is not risen, our preaching is in vain and your faith is in vain
. . . But Christ is risen, the first-fruits of those that were dead."
That which has been preached, wherein they stand and
whereby they are saved, is *that which has taken place in history,* the unique event of the Gospel story, the inrush of God
into history: He who has been among us and whom we have
seen and touched with our hands.

So, Christianity is built on fact, is witness to a fact; but
it is not only something based on fact. It is the preaching of
an historical fact (which was, at the same time, mystical
Presence) and simultaneously the being laid hand upon, even
now, *by His Presence,* the invisible but most real Presence of
the Glorified Lord *even now among us*: "And lo, I am with
you always, even unto the end of the world" (Matthew
28:20); "Not I live, Christ lives in me" (Gal. 2:20). Historical fact and mystical Presence—Presence among us and

possessing us even now—that is the characteristic feature of Christianity.

Both this fact and mystical Presence, which are in an indissoluble way united together, are the opening of the gates of His mercy, the manifestation of His *boundless condescension,* the inrush and revelation of the active, saving, self-humiliating, self-sacrificing, boundlessly condescending Love of God (cf. John 3:16 and I John 4:10). *This* is peculiar to the Christian message: an historical fact, an historical Person . . . and in this Person "all the plenitude of the Godhead dwelling bodily" (Col. 2:9) and in this fact, the salvation and sanctification of the world, the victory over the powers of death and evil.

But the victory—let us repeat it again and again—has been achieved on the Cross; and His Cross is not only the supreme revelation of the boundless condescending Love of God, but also the center, the backbone and pivot of our own new life. We enter this new life only by participating in the Cross of Christ, crucifying thereon our "old Adam" and partaking in the perfect obedience of Christ. Christianity is therefore much more than a message: it is a new reality, a new life, a painful and courageous transfiguration of the old man into the "new creature," into a "member of the body of Christ." "The old things have passed away. Behold! Everything has become new!" It is a promise and a beginning of—let us repeat it—a *New Reality,* already revealed and given to us in the coming, the death and the resurrection of Christ, which are the "leaven" of the new order of being. This leaven has to permeate the whole lump.

Therefore, the sense of the "fulfillment" that has already taken place ("It is fulfilled!") is most organically, in an indissoluble way, connected in Christianity with the expectation of the future total revelation of the glory when God will be "all in all" (I Cor. 15). In so hoping, we are eagerly "stretching forward"; but this stretching forward cannot be separated, on the other hand, from the sense of mystical possession, of intimate union: the Treasure is here, is given. We are bearers thereof, although in "earthen vessels." However, we do not possess: *Christ takes hold of us.* "Not I live, Christ lives in me," "Christ has to be glorified in me, be it in life or in death." Therefore, "I have decided to know nothing except Christ, and Him crucified," for here is the center, the spring, of the New Reality.

The world still "lies in wickedness," but the victory has been *won already*. In the final revelation of the power of God, in the Lord's second and final triumphant coming this will be wholly manifested. However, this victory—through death and resurrection—is already the backbone and the substance of the message: "Be of good cheer: I have overcome the world."

PART II

7

Suffering

1.

The world is continuously passing away, and we long for something that is immutable. But perhaps even more than by this passing away, we feel baffled by the mystery of suffering. Is it necessary? It surrounds us on all sides, we meet it at every step. We are simply intruded upon by the news, the impression of suffering rushing upon us from every quarter, *e.g.* out of the daily newspaper: with so many persons burnt alive, so many drowned, so many dashed to pieces in an air-crash. We are really at a loss how to understand the meaning of all that, how to accept it, how to be reconciled with this course of life, this order of the universe, where such things can and do happen continuously. We feel we cannot agree with that; we are filled with horror; we are struck dumb; we are full of an internal protest. We are overwhelmed by those images of people being butchered, being imprisoned in concentration camps against all human right, submitted to the most cruel, cynical and refined tortures, both physical and moral, all those unspeakable horrors taking place during our lifetime, at a distance of so and so many thousand miles from us. How can we remain indifferent to all that? But people in Europe are not even separated by thousands of miles from these scenes of slaughter. Many among them have personally passed through such experiences, having watched it from near or having escaped a similar fate by sheer miracle. Human bodies carbonized and unrecognizable, towns and

villages burned out and destroyed, millions of human lives
crippled and maimed, the fruits of many centuries of human
labor and culture brutally annihilated, recklessness and feroc-
ity of tyrants and conquerors reigning and thriving—all this
is a part not only of a recent and still fresh historical past,
not only of a terrible yesterday, but also of the present-day
world situation. How are we to understand all this? And then
the groans and the death-rattle in all our hospitals throughout all countries, and the torments of those who by an
incurable disease are doomed to a painful death—how are
we to explain this also, how are we to imagine that God has
willed it, that God has agreed to it?

Our hearts are faltering with pity, and wincing under the
thought of those torments suffered by others. But are we
more compassionate than God? How then can He allow such
things to happen? This is the most troubling question which
can be put to our religious conscience. Let us try to realize
the full scope of this problem and to feel the acuity of the
point and to seek to answer. An answer does not always mean
an explanation; and vice versa: a plausible and smooth
theoretical explanation can sometimes prove quite inadequate
to quench the trouble of the heart, to satisfy its desire, its
craving for peace and for justice. I believe that only the
manifestation of a Higher Reality might prove to be adequate,
to be able to cope with this problem, to give a satisfying
answer, if answer there be: only a contact with God, an encounter with God. Christianity says: an encounter with the
Suffering God.

2.

The Christian answer is the message about the Suffering
God, or rather more than that: His *really having come* to
share our sufferings unto the depths of death, and that on the
Cross. This sheds new light on the whole question, and not
only on this question, but on the whole reality of the world's
life. There is no explanation coming first; there is this fact
coming first: He is sharing our sufferings, He is hallowing

our sufferings by His Presence, by His participation therein.
Here there is no explanation, but rather a new revelation,
something totally new, astonishing, incomprehensible, taking
us totally aback, paradoxical and unexpected, and—true. Here
lies the answer, not the theoretical answer (I mean, in first
place) but the practical, the real solution of the problem. His
death and His suffering on the Cross are the real solution of
the problem.

God proves Himself to be of boundless, unthinkable,
unfathomable and active mercy, of selfless, self-sacrificing
condescension. He is not only compassionate, but also much
more: the Son of God dies for our sake, in order to save us
and to hallow our dying and our suffering.

Is this an answer? Yes, I think, it is: because we are not
alone, not left alone. Even in our being left alone we have
Him with us, sharing our being left alone, in this cry of
death-agony: "My God, My God, wherefore hast Thou forsaken Me?" Death and torments can mean that He bears
company with us; they become His Presence and His Fellowship with us. We have here a new vital center, a new spiritual
—and very real—Reality. But how difficult does it usually
seem for us to attain it!

3.

There are two different approaches to the problem of
suffering from the Christian point of view, and both are necessary. Yea, more than that: they are, from this Christian
point of view, most intimately connected with one another.

The first approach is to be deeply struck, deeply haunted
by the sufferings of the fellow-men, and even more—by the
suffering of all creatures. Isaac of Syria, perhaps the greatest
among the ascetic and mystical writers of Eastern Christianity,
speaks of this immense compassion which takes hold of a
heart that approaches the summits of perfection. "What is a
compassionate heart?" he asks, and he answers:

It is a kindling of the heart for all creation—for mankind, the birds, the animals, even the enemies of the truth and for all that is. And when he thinks of them or contemplates them, tears stream from his eyes because of the power of mercy which moves his heart with great compassion. And the heart feels itself touched, and he cannot endure to see or hear a creature suffer any harm, even the slightest pain. And he offers then, even for those who hurt him, continuous prayers and tears, that they might be saved and strengthened. Even for those that creep in the dust does he pray—out of the immense compassion which is poured out into his heart without measure, following the example of God.

We are taken aback; we are shaken by the suffering of our brethren. We cannot reconcile ourselves to it. We have to help them as much as we can. Our fate in the future world will depend on the share of love shown by us to them: "Because you have done it to one of those least among My brethren, you have done it to Me." We see the presence of the suffering Christ in our suffering brethren. And if we cannot help them by a visible external action, if we cannot alleviate their suffering with our own means, we can and we must intercede for them, implore God for them with all the strength of our heart, with all the burning of our love, as Isaac of Syria depicts it: incessant prayer, knocking at the door of His mercy. No rest, no self-complacent relaxation, but go on knocking, with the firm trust that He will hear, that He will save. No cool-hearted philosophy at the expense of our fellow-man, no being reconciled with the sufferings of the brethren. Instead, crying to the Lord, imploring His mercy.

On the other hand, there are some glimpses of the general, the ultimate meaning and sense of suffering, glimpses vouchsafed to us directly in our own experience, *through our own suffering.* Unknown depths and realities are suddenly opened before us, and we come to see and feel things which we never suspected before. The Son of God Himself in His agony at the garden of Gethsemane prayed to His Father, that this cup might pass from Him, but He added: "but not as I will,

but as Thou wilt." And it is only natural for us—it is even the
normal attitude—that we should pray God to relieve us from
suffering and misfortunes and sorrow. But we are led to guess
and to feel and to recognize more: the will of God, which is
behind the suffering and is speaking to us, addressing us
directly through it. Concerning the brethren we must continue
asking God to relieve them. Here, in our own case, it is only
natural that we pray God to relieve us from the evils; but
more is required from us: we have to listen to the will of God
speaking to us even through our sufferings—and perhaps
especially strongly through our sufferings—and be ready to
submit to it: "Thy will be done!" "Not as I will, but as Thou
wilt." And here we come near to the center of the Christian
revelation, of the revealed mystery: the sense of life, the sense
of the whole of history is given in the voluntary suffering
of the Son of God, in the total submission of His will—
"obedient unto death, even the death on the Cross"—to the
will of the Father.

Once we have accepted our lot as coming from God and
have bowed to His will, an unexpected force which we could
not imagine or think of can stream into us and support and
comfort us amidst horrors and pains. And then we can even
come to feel the bliss of bowing to His will. Yea, more than
that: the bliss of sharing the passion and the agony and the
self-sacrifice of the Son of God. And this is not words only.
This can—and must—become a *reality,* as we have many examples thereof. And this gives sense and meaning to our
suffering: if it becomes a part of His suffering, by our freely
accepting it.

4.

We often cannot—and we need not—understand the ways
of God. We are often deeply struck down by the burden of
woe and sorrow which has fallen upon us. But already in the
Old Testament, Job rightly felt where the solution of our
painful bewilderment lies. No explanations are given in the
Book of Job for the woes and catastrophes which have struck

him down with the permission of God. The only answer
given in the book to the cries and dramatic questions of Job
is the Divine Reality, is the manifestation and *Presence of
God.* No other answer can be given to us. But in the Christian
revelation, the Divine Reality has become incomparably more
manifested and the Presence has drawn nearer and is more
comforting and more adequate to our needs: it is *the Presence
of the Suffering God,* it is the Only-Begotten Son of God who
has become—in a most real and perfect way—our brother and
has entered the abyss of our suffering. You remember how
Dostoevsky is seized with horror in contemplating the picture
of general suffering throughout the world; but especially the
picture of the suffering of the innocent, in first place that of
little children, baffles him. If this is the price which has to
be paid for the future harmony, then *we cannot accept this
harmony,* we cannot afford to pay the price, says Ivan Karamazov. The only answer which the other brother, Aloysha
(representing Dostoevsky's own faith and attitude), can give,
is the image of the Crucified: He can pardon all, He can
reconcile all, for He has measured the depth of our afflictions,
of our loneliness, of our pain. Through Him, through His
death on the Cross, the ways of God are justified; God is
justified in His creation of the world. For here, in this suffering, the ultimate sense, the ultimate background of all life
has become apparent: the boundless love of God, as the essential, the primordial and final meaning—even of suffering.
For now suffering means the most intimate union with Him,
even in pain and death. And that means: Life Eternal.

There is a very profound and indeed mysterious saying of
the Apostle Paul's in the Epistle to Colossians: "Now I am
rejoicing in my suffering for you, and I fill up that which is
lacking of the afflictions of Christ in my flesh for His Body's
sake, which is the Church" (1:24). We hear often and much
in Paul's writings of the intimate union with the suffering
Lord, with the Cross and the death of Christ, of "co-crucifixion" with Christ as the only means to attain the "newness
of life," Life Eternal. It is the chief contents of Paul's preaching, the summary of his experience and doctrine, his ideal of
life: "I am crucified with Christ, and I don't live any more—

Christ lives in me" (Gal. 2:20). Or: "We always bear about
the dying of the Lord Jesus, that the life also of Jesus might
be made manifest in our body" (II Cor. 4:10). But here, in
this passage from Colossians, something even more mysterious
and startling is said. Not only can we share in the suffering
of Christ, but more than that: our suffering can become *His;*
our suffering, having become a part of His suffering, can
become a *part of His work of salvation,* for the good of our
brethren. But ours is not the merit, the patience, the obedience, the redeeming force. It is His; but it can work in us
and, more than that, even through us, for the benefit of
others. His blessed, world-redeeming passion thus is working
in us and through us.

5.

When we have reached this stage—of obedient and humble
self-surrender to our Lord—then we can also deliver our
brethren into His arms, surrender them to His guardianship
and guidance and love, knowing then what it means to find
Him and to have Him, be it even in suffering. But *we cannot
accept the Cross for others,* on behalf of others; we can do
it only for ourselves. Some theoreticians of Christianity are
sometimes too inclined to accept the Cross for others. This
is impossible and impious. But, as the depths of a new life
are revealed to us in the Cross, so we may guess and hope and
trust, in humility and trembling, praying God for the deliverance or the strengthening of our brethren, that our brethren
also will not be left alone, that our Lord will comfort them
also and reveal His blissful Presence to them, even in suffering.
The ultimate sense of existence—even of suffering—dawns
on us. But let us not be theoreticians, but humble and loving,
patient in our own trials, tireless in our prayer and in our
work for the relief of our brethren from their pains and
troubles. Then we shall here again suddenly be faced with
this comforting and great mystery: His Presence. "I was
hungry, and you gave Me to eat. I was thirsty, and you slaked

my thirst. I was a homeless stranger, and you received Me; naked, and you clothed Me. I was sick, and you visited Me. I was in jail, and you came to Me" (Matt. 25: 35-36). His Presence is here—in the suffering brethren, crowning them with a new dignity. That is the practical Christian attitude towards the problem of suffering; and it reveals hidden mysteries and depths of love—His love!—in us and through us and in Him. And that is the answer: His hidden and manifested love, revealed to us in glimpses—in His life, His death and resurrection, and also in the sharing of His Cross and in the gift and grace of compassion given to us. His love, "taking hold of us," this love, stronger than death and suffering, manifested on the Cross, is the answer. That answer is not theoretical; it is *dynamical*—and creative. It transfigures suffering and life and all that is.

8

The Meaning and Goal of History

1.

Is there a sense in the historical process? Do we see and recognize it? If we do, it is only partially, in a very insufficient way. We see (I mean, if we believe in God—if we believe in God as manifested in Jesus Christ) only glimpses of this ultimate meaning, only hints pointing to it, dimly and hazily imperfect hints. The mass and the maze of the individual facts as to their ultimate sense escapes our understanding. So what we see is only a ray of light in darkness, but a ray of light which is perhaps sufficient to guide us.

It is clear that the meaning and sense of history depends on the end or the goal towards which it moves. If the end is only a catastrophe, or a series of repeated catastrophes, a destruction of all life, the falling into pieces of our universe, then of course no sense whatever is given. For a sense that is engulfed by nothingness, by utter destruction and chaos, is no sense at all. If there is a sense, it must be a deeper sense, rooted deeper, rooted in Something that is beyond destruction, that remains safe and unshaken and immutable. But is there a Something that remains untouched by the process of permanent passing away of all things, by their rushing into the abyss of annihilation? In other words, is the image of the world as familiar to us and as open to scientific investigation really *all* that exists, or—to put it better—is it really that which the world really is? All these innumerable worlds and systems of worlds, all subject to falling asunder, to decomposition and to destruction: are they the real world, the real face of Reality? Or are they perhaps only a shadow—certainly strongly substantiated, certainly very well-founded (compare the *phaenomenon bene fundatum* of Leibnitz)—*projected* before our eyes and mind? Perhaps the destruction, the falling asunder, the flowing away, the being engulfed without possible escape in the abyss . . . concerns only the shadow; and the real Reality is not touched thereby or is touched only indirectly (as far as the Reality may be interested even in the destiny of its projected shadow). That of course would change the whole outlook: if there is no final destruction of all that is, then of course there is a sense, a meaning, a goal, even in the changes of the shadow projected by the Reality that stands beyond it.

Do we mean thereby only the Divine Reality? Or is there also a *real face of things,* concealed to us, of which we only get—and that rarely—a few glimpses, but turned towards God? If so, this ultimate face of things cannot be utterly destroyed, because God has created it and God sustains it. In God it has its source of being, and God will "deliver it from its bondage to corruption into the freedom and glory of the children of God." If so, then there is an indestructible and abiding sense and meaning of History, in spite of all the cataclysms, in spite of the most radical and total destruction. These things do not concern the inward face, the inward being of things, the inward being of the universe, which remains standing before the face of God. And hereupon the ultimate sense of History is grounded.

2.

The real face, the real essence of things—that is, in the Christian conception—although founded and harbored in God, is in a process of becoming, of an historical becoming which comprises the fall, the ascension, the reintegration and the restoration of man and the universe. The march of the movement is Godwards, but not on a direct line, as perhaps it could be and was meant to be. It is an ascension, a rehabilitation after a catastrophe, after a spiritual catastrophe. This is the Christian idea, the Christian scheme of history: a tending to God, in weakness and imperfection, after a fall, or rather only a dim longing and groping for God with virtually no power to attain Him, and then—redemption, help, new life coming *from God* through the inrush of *God Himself* into history, into the very texture of our life, of our destiny and our being. This is the *oikonomia,* the "household-plan" of God, according to Paul. And then begins the way homewards, in manly strife and struggle against spiritual foes, the way of ascension: through sharing in the Cross and in the victory of the Son of God who became man. So the history of man and that of the world is full of tension and drama. And there is dramatism behind the screen of visible history, a greater dramatism than we are aware of—on the level of spiritual Reality. Thus we see a drama, a struggle and a victory: a victory that has been already won but which is not fully realized in all its consequences because it still has to work as a "leaven" in the historical process and in the life of the cosmos.

The spiritual drama and the catastrophe, the fall, explains the projection of the "shadow." This "shadowy" or rather fallen world is very real, and the Evil that reigns therein, and the process of dying and of suffering and of flowing away, is very real; but that does not affect the ultimate roots of the world, the face that is turned toward God. The real and ultimate essence of the world is still fettered by the "bondage of corruption," but this "bondage of corruption" is not the last word, just as it has not been the primordial one, for the "bondage of corruption" has been already overcome by the victory of the Son of God.

So history is a drama, not only in "cosmical" dimensions, on a cosmical level, but much more than that: in spiritual dimensions, on a spiritual level which goes beyond the cosmical and is the root thereof. Yet history, this drama, is not a phantasmagoria. The spiritual level on which this real drama of history is developing is very real, and the "shadow" projected in our so-called reality is also real, although of a derivative reality. So the meaning, the sense of history is in the spiritual strife which, affecting also the outward world, in fact is going on in this outward world and centering in the redemption. And the redemption redeems the world in all its dimensions and has really taken place on our earth, because the Word of God became flesh and offered Himself in obedience to the Father and really died on the Cross and really rose from the physical death in His real, but glorified human body. And now the forces of this redemption are working in the world and shaping history. Therefore the word "shadow" for our physical world, which we have used in this chapter, is inadequate and misleading. It was useful to us, in showing the derivative character of the so-called world, but it is inadequate, because it does not sufficiently stress its reality, be it only a derivative one. So we see the purport of the drama is spiritual *and* outward, concrete, historical; it is spiritual *and* physical as well. And the fate of the physical cosmos, of our physical earth, of our physical and psychical civilization is not something despicable and unimportant (so it would be from an ultra-idealistic or an ultra-mystical, acosmic point of view), but on the contrary, of the utmost importance for the general meaning and trend of the world drama: *instaurare omnia in Christum,* to subject all things under His feet. The goal of the world drama is the ultimate victory of God and the free ultimate subjection and surrender of all creation to God through man. But this victory of God concerns all the elements, all the aspects, all the stages and levels of the creation.

The sense of history is the final decisive release of this world—in this its fallen, "cosmical" aspect—from bondage to corruption. That is also the ultimate sense of all that was and is going on before our eyes on our earth, because all the struggles and politics on earth are the reflection of the spiritual strife or of the degradation of the creature and its "bondage." The aim of this human history is and was to outstep itself, which aim has become possible by the breaking through of Life Eternal into history. The meaning of history can be therefore measured by its relation to the Life Eternal which broke through into history, and by its relation to the ultimate goal, *i.e.,* the supreme and full manifestation of this victory and plenitude of Life Eternal, which has become flesh and has "lived among us" (ἐσκήνωσεν ἐν ἡμῖν).

3.

The Christian philosophy of history is conceived *from a center*, from a definite, concrete center. In the "fulness of time" (τὸ πλήρωμα τοῦ χρόνου, Gal. 4:4) God has been revealed in flesh in an unique and decisive way, sanctifying soul and body, the whole texture of life, giving a center, a sense and a goal to the whole process of history. From the Christian point of view there is no senselessness in history. All parts of the historical periphery are in some relation—however obscure and invisible it be to us—to the central event of the world's history: the incarnation, the suffering and the victory of the Divine Logos.

In older times there were in ancient religions dim forebodings, yea even expectations of the coming decisive fact of human—and also cosmical—history. The pagan religions in their glimpses of truth, which are deeply interwoven with masses of sometimes the most repulsive superstitions, in those scattered glimpses and rays of Truth—those religions, I say, are pointing towards something beyond them. So are also, to a large extent, the deeply moving philosophical and religious yearnings of many ancient religious thinkers. It is not for nothing that the Christian writers Justin the Philosopher and Clement of Alexandria spoke of the "seeds of the Divine Logos" scattered through the world and operating in the hearts of Socrates and Heraclitus. From the Christian point of view, if there is a real redemption that has taken place in history, all in history before and after that fact must stand in some connection therewith, be it positive or negative. It is the inspiring moving force of history. As depicted in those beautiful old Advent chants of the Latin Church, there is a yearning that runs through the history of mankind, the history of our earth, the yearning for the coming of the Savior; and His coming is an answer from Above to this yearning: *Rorate coeli desuper . . . Aperiatur terra, et germinat Salvatorem!*

The Christian has the right to consider all previous development in the history of mankind as "preparation for the
Gospel"—*praeparatio evangelica*—as it has been formulated
by an ancient Church writer. "Lo, I send My messenger before
Thy face in order to prepare Thy way before Thee." These
words of the prophet Malachi, applied by the Gospel-writers
to designate the role of John the Baptist, could be used also
in a wider sense. A Russian religious philosopher, a great
Christian also—Prince Serge Troubetzkoy, dedicated his life
to the tracing out of the presentiments in the ancient world
of the revelation of the Divine Logos. The difference between
the religious ideas, the religious experiences of the ancient
pre-Christian world and the Christian revelation is an immense one. But the chief difference is not on the plane of ideas
only. It is much more than that: here, in the Christian revelation, we have the *fulfillment,* the fulfillment of the plan of
God, the fulfillment of the best and highest yearnings of
mankind. Τετέλεσται, "it is consummated": those last words
uttered by Christ on the Cross, according to the Fourth Gospel
(19:30), can be written as an epigraph over the whole apostolic message. What the kings and prophets wanted to see
and to hear and could not, now is here, among us. "Blessed
are therefore your eyes and your ears!" For the Bridegroom is
here among us, the Kingdom of Heaven is near at hand, yea,
it is amidst you. The Plenitude has been revealed: "In Him
all the Plenitude of God abode corporally" (Col. 2:9). So
the whole historical outlook, all the historical valuations are
changed; they are conditioned by their relation to the Plenitude that has been revealed. The flow of time is no longer a
return of the same numberless circles, neither is it a being
engulfed by the abyss of mutability into which the stream
rushes down without halt, hopelessly, irretrievably. This flow
of time becomes rather a streaming forth towards God, a
hallowing of the earthly and the created by the leaven of the
Divine, by the Divine Plenitude that entered our earthly life
and history and gave sense to history.

4.

If the incarnation of the Logos of God is the center for all past and present history, it is also the central fact deciding the future. The Christian expectation of the end, of the final and decisive consummation of the victory of God, is a most inalienable part of the Christian message. We know what an immense role eschatological hopes and expectations played in primitive Christianity. There has been a very strong tendency among many theologians of the first part of the 20th century to ascribe to eschatology such a predominant place in the primitive Christian outlook that all other aspects thereof become obscured. There was a tendency to oppose the "mystical" sense of the Divine Presence to eschatology as two different currents in early Christian faith and experience. Nothing could be more unjustified. Both elements are in the closest way connected with one another; they are two sides of one experience. It is the overpowering experience of the redeeming action of God, of the "household-plan" of God (οἰκονομία τοῦ Θεοῦ), the outflow of His immense and boundless bounty, in which all has been foreseen—also our freedom which is included in this plan, which is one of the pivots of this plan—and where all the obstacles to its fulfillment turn out at the end to be instruments for the greater manifestation of the all-overcoming majesty and justice and lovingkindness of God. This plan necessarily connects past, present and future, because it bridges over the whole process. So without the ultimate revelation of His glory and His victory, the plan and the redeeming action of God remains uncompleted. But more than that: the experience of the "immense riches" given in Christ, the boundless "love of Christ" that "transcends all understanding," takes hold of us. It is a mystical overflow in which all is submerged by this supreme boon, supreme possession: Christ—even in pain and suffering, nay, especially in pain and suffering. But this overflow *asks for more and more*: for a still closer connection, a still greater surrender, a still more intimate union with Christ. "I have the desire to be released [from life] and to be with Christ," says Paul, although the same Paul had already proclaimed: "Not I live forthwith, but Christ lives in me." This experience of the living union with Christ cries for still greater consummation, for a perfection which takes hold of our body as well as of our soul. We are called to take part in His risen life, and we are expecting with yearning the coming fulness of manifestation of His glory and His power, so "that this body of our humiliation should become like unto the body of His glory." "We are moaning, desiring for sonship and for the redemption of our body."

The mystical overflow—in the earnestness and sobriety of co-crucifixion with Christ—demands completeness of union with Christ. Thus the mystical experience is the necessary presupposition of Christian eschatology. And the redemption is not perfect if it does not work in us and in the whole creation till "all the creature is liberated from bondage to corruption into the freedom and glory of the children of God." Eschatological tension and mystical possession complete each other, they are necessary links of *one* experience. My mystical union with Christ has to reshape me completely, also my mortal body, and demands as its necessary completion the total and final victory and presence of God, "God all in all." There is no Christianity without this expectation. As there is no Christianity without the acceptance of the *historical* revelation of God, of the historical facts in which God has been revealed—I mean the central and unique revelation of the Divine Logos that became Flesh—, so likewise there is no Christian faith and Christian outlook without the fervent hope for the coming plenitude of the revelation of God, which means that the historical process, the household-plan of God concerning the whole of creation shall attain its perfection, its fulfillment—on the bosom of the Heavenly Father. That is the meaning and the goal of history: the travelling home—not only of us, but of the whole creation— and . . . *final transfiguration*. But the decisive victory of God has already been won, and that in history.

9

Resurrection and Transfiguration

1.

The Resurrection is, according to Christian belief, not only the crowning of Christ's whole work and earthly life, it is not only the great proof, the testimony given by God, it is more than that: it is the very center and the very essence of the Christian Gospel.[1] It is the beginning of a new life, of a new Reality, or rather the inrush, the revelation of Life Eternal. Life Eternal entered into the texture of our life and manifested itself therein and conquered death. The new Reality reveals itself as a transfiguring Power. If we listen to the Gospel narratives concerning the apparitions of the Risen One, we cannot but notice that we have to do here with glimpses of a higher plane of life which is only adumbrated, which cannot be fully apprehended by us. It is not a phantasmagoria, not a vision; it is concrete, not an abstraction, not an idea; it is a higher *Reality*. He eats before them; He invites Thomas to touch Him; He is recognized by the two disciples in the breaking of the bread. Not a phantom, not a ghost is speaking to them—He Himself emphasizes that.[2] It is a concrete, living Person: the beloved Master. And yet a change has taken place. We breathe in those passages—even more than in other passages of the Gospel—the air of Life Eternal: of the Life that has triumphed over death, an air of

[1]See also my German book, *Die Verklärung der Welt und des Lebens* (Bertelmann, Gütersloh, 1955).
[2]Luke 29:38-40.

107

enhanced Reality, mighty, earnest and peaceful. In John 20:19-28, we read:

> Then the same day at evening, being the first day of the week, when the doors were shut where the disciples were assembled for fear of the Jews, Jesus came and stood in the midst, and saith unto them, Peace be unto you. And when He had said, He showed unto them His hands and His side. Then were the disciples glad, when they saw the Lord.

> Then said Jesus to them again, Peace be unto you: as my Father hath sent me, even so send I you. And when He had said this, He breathed on them, and saith unto them, Receive ye the Holy Spirit: Whosoever sins ye remit, they are remitted unto them; and whosoever sins ye retain, they are retained.

> But Thomas, one of the twelve, called Didymus, was not with them when Jesus came. The other disciples therefore said unto him, We have seen the Lord. But he said unto them, Except I shall see in His hands the print of the nails, and put my finger into the print of the nails, and thrust my hands into His side, I will not believe.

> And after eight days again His disciples were within, and Thomas with them: then came Jesus, the doors being shut, and stood in the midst, and said, Peace be unto you. Then saith He to Thomas, Reach hither thy finger, and behold my hands; and reach hither thy hand, and thrust it into my side: and be not faithless, but believing. And Thomas answered and said unto Him, My Lord and my God.

In Luke also we have this feeling of an enhanced Reality connected with the appearances of the Risen Lord (24:30-43):

> And it came to pass, as He sat at meat with them [the

two disciples at Emmaus], He took bread and blessed it, and brake, and gave to them. And their eyes were opened, and they knew Him; and He vanished out of their sight. And they said one to another, Did not our heart burn within us, while He talked with us by the way, and while He opened to us the scriptures?

And they rose up the same hour, and returned to Jerusalem, and found the eleven gathered together, and them that were with them, saying, The Lord is risen indeed, and hath appeared to Simon. And they told what things were done in the way, and how He was known of them in breaking of bread.

And as they thus spoke, Jesus Himself stood in the midst of them, and saith unto them, Peace be unto you. But they were terrified and affrighted, and supposed that they had seen a spirit. And He said to them. Why are ye troubled? and why do thoughts arise in your hearts? Behold my hands and my feet, that it is I myself: handle me, and see: for a spirit hath not flesh and bones, as ye see me have.

And when He had thus spoken, He showed them His hands and His feet.

And while they yet believed not for joy, and wondered, He said unto them, Have ye here any meat? And they gave Him a piece of a broiled fish, and of a honeycomb. And He took it, and did eat before them.

In Matthew they fall down before Him (chapter 28) and He says: "All power is given unto Me in heaven and earth."

The additional, twenty-first chapter of John—with the appearance of the Lord to the disciples at the sea of Tiberias and the threefold reintegration of Peter in his dignity of apostle, and with Peter and the "disciple whom Jesus loved" following the Master—is also permeated by the sense of the overpowering Presence of the Risen One. And this meal on

the shore of the lake—"Jesus then cometh and taketh bread
and giveth them, and fish likewise" (v. 13)—is there not,
just as in the story of the disciples of Emmaus, a tinge of a
eucharistic meaning about it? Thus the Gospel narratives
about the Risen Lord and His factual corporal appearances to
them seem to lead to the experience of His eucharistic Presence, the Presence of the Glorified One—the Same who had
suffered and vanquished death—and to be already combined
therewith.

It is a new atmosphere of triumphant Life Eternal, not an
abstraction, not a denial, but—as we said already—an enhance-
ment, yea, a transfiguration of earthly life, that has already
begun in the Person of Christ.

This reality of the Resurrection, this new life of the Risen
One, is the basis on which Christianity rose. It is so, both historically and essentially. They had all fled; Peter had denied
Him thrice: only the Mother and the disciple "whom Jesus
loved" and some pious compassionate women stood by the
foot of the Cross. They were in deep discouragement and
depression; they did not believe the women who first brought
the news of the Resurrection: they sit behind locked doors
"out of fear of the Jews." These disheartened and mourning
men were utterly unable to propagate a new religion, to
proclaim the victory of Life Eternal. Something must have
taken place that changed totally their whole attitude towards
life and their whole surrounding, something that inspired
them with overwhelming joyous certainty. It was *their encounter* with the Risen One and their being taken hold of by
the streams of Life Eternal revealed in Him and coming forth
from Him. The central theme of Christian preaching is—
Resurrection. We know it from Acts, we know it from early
Christian prayers, we know it from Paul's epistles.

Something new has stepped in and has changed the whole
outlook. This is what explains this tone of unrivaled joy and
certainty, this tone of victory that permeates the whole. "This
is the victory that has vanquished the world—even our faith."
Not words, but a reality, decisive, conquering and overwhelming. Here we touch the vital nerve of the Christian message,
of the Christian witness. They don't preach any theories, be

it philosophical, moral or mystical. They bear witness to a *fact*. That is why they are preaching: "we cannot but bear witness of what we have heard and seen." And this fact is: Victory of Life Eternal, Victory over Death, the Resurrection. A glimpse is given of what Life Eternal really is—and that is the risen Life of Christ. A new process of regeneration and rehabilitation has been started, which will continue until all be saved, redeemed, engulfed in Life Eternal. The whole creation will be therefore freed from the bondage of corruption into the freedom and glory of the children of God. The "eternal burden of glory" is already working in us and is transforming, transfiguring us.

Resurrection means Transfiguration, essential, decisive Transfiguration. And Transfiguration is the distant goal, the distant vision and dream to which mankind tends. But here the dream has become reality; the distant goal entered history and became the new creative center of history. The Resurrection, the breaking through of the victorious reality of Life Eternal, is the real event that fulfilled the dreams and visions of mankind.

2.

The yearning for a transfigured life, for a transfigured world—that is the secret meaning of many human yearnings, that is also the ultimate meaning of art. Real art means becoming aware—not theoretically, but in an instinctive, unconscious way—of this hidden transfigured reality and to communicate the vision thereof—by hints, by sounds and words and colors. There is unconscious, hidden metaphysics in great art. True art is not didactic in its essence; it does not want to prove. It just sees and feels; it is haunted and subjugated, and it tries to reproduce this. It feels itself drawn with force into unknown depths of life. The poet speaks then of "mysterious valleys" (Pushkin), of "fairy isles of sunny lawn," of "enchanted mountains and caves of divine sleep" (Shelley), of "gentle tones of harp floating in the air of spring" (Möricke), of a "sonorous solitude" and "silent music" ("la musica

callada," "la solidad sonora": John of the Cross). This state
of silent concentration opening sudden vistas on the intense
interior life of the surrounding world, on the depths of this
life, is thus depicted by Wordsworth:

> . . . we became a living soul
> While with an eye made quiet by the power
> Of harmony and the deep power of joy,
> We see into the life of things.

There is a beauty that sometimes takes hold of the soul
with a force of obsession and the soul quivers to its touch.
It is sometimes more than it can bear, more than it can stand.
This feeling is well known to Shelley. The flowers in the
enchanted garden are languishing under the sweet burden of
joy and beauty streaming upon them from all sides. The world
seems illuminated and transfigured.

> The pluméd insects swift and free,
> Like golden boats on a sunny sea,
> Laden with light and odour, which pass
> Over the gleam of the living grass;
> The unseen clouds of the dew which lie
> Like fire in the flowers till the sun rides high,
> They wander like spirits among the spheres,
> Each cloud faint with the fragrance it bears;
> The quivering vapours of dim noontide,
> Which like a sea o'er the warm earth glide,
> In which every sound, and odour and beam
> Move like reeds in a single stream . . . (Shelley)

This is a picture of that enhanced beauty, alive in the
quiet tension of the noontide hours, that takes hold of the
poet's soul. It subjugates; it attracts with overpowering
might.

> Throw yourself, keen and breathing freedom,
> In this life-giving ocean's depth.
>   (the great Russian lyric poet Tiutchev)

In the experience of the great painters and in their master-pieces there is often a hidden beauty of simple, average everyday objects revealed to the artist's and the onlooker's eyes. There appears a deep connection with a greater context, a being rooted in this greater context, in the secret depths of life. This being rooted in those secret depths is what permeates the most simple, unpretentious landscape and what constitutes its beauty. A flowering bush, a birchtree in the middle of a field, a thatched cottage on a hill, a vast stretch of corn-fields or lawns—there can be an immense beauty in it. I will not build up metaphysical theories here, but it seems that artistic beauty points to a subconscious dim perception of a hidden larger context, of the secret roots of things; and this dim perception of this silent living context, this listening to the silent voices, to this intense living silence, transfigures with beauty.

Of course this artistic transfiguration by the power of beauty, even if it corresponds to some hidden secret background of things, is utterly insufficient, not to say illusionary. It does not last, and it does not actually redeem. It transfigures *our perception* of things, this new perception most probably standing in some connection to their hidden background, but not their concrete fate, their mutability, their imperfection, their passing away and, in the case of living and feeling creatures, their suffering. This transfiguration is aesthetical. It reflects, it reveals life connecting it with its hidden contents, but it does not change life, it *does not create life* renewed and free from evil.

3.

There are other channels and means besides art to experience a kind of transfigured life, be it a very limited and circumscribed area. A thing of immense value and sanctity in the history of man was and is the family and family-life. It was and is felt not only as part of everyday life illuminated by the power of mutual affection, of radiating love, the mother being the great focus of this love, but also—in pagan religions as well as in Christianity—as an area of life where the influxes of divine energies, of a divine presence were especially felt. In paganism the forces of natural growth, the saps of life, the mystery of sexual union and of procreation were by themselves considered as divine. In the Christian outlook and experience those natural, created things have to become, by the power of God's grace, bearers of a higher life, have to be uplifted in a higher sphere of spiritual reality, conserving at the same time their natural, earthly features, but sanctified and purified. We know how strongly *e.g.* the ancient Romans felt the sanctity of the home, centered in the sanctity of the hearth. The presence of invisible forces—the god protectors of the house—was felt especially in the nearness of the hearth. Ovid thus speaks of olden times, when all members of the household were sitting for the meal at long tables before the sacred fire of the hearth with the pious belief that the gods also took part in the meal:

> Ante focos olim scamnis considere longia
> Mos erat et mensae credere adesse deos
> (Fasti VI, 290).

An atmosphere of awe and reverence permeated family life in those pious pagan homes. The natural ties of family affection were enhanced and fostered by the religious background. We find the same thing in pious Chinese and Indian homes. So much the more was the atmosphere of pious Christian families deeply penetrated by the sense of the nearness of the Divine. A profoundly believing, God-fearing Christian family was as if it were a little organic cell of church life, a "house-church" (cf. I Cor. 16: 9). But the Christian transfiguration of life, of the family atmosphere, of the home stretches and tends farther: the earthly home is but an image, and anticipation of the Home Eternal.

The first rays of pure youthful love can transfigure, in the eyes of those who love the whole surrounding scenery, the simplest event of life, the whole texture of life with a glamour of beauty, with the shine of the beloved Presence. We see this *e.g.* in the sonnets of Dante, in some love poems of Petrarca, of the marvellous German romanticist Eichendorff and other poets. And how the world becomes illuminated, shining, full of mysterious, entrancing, enticing promise to the eyes of youth in general, to this stretching out of the young soul, full of fresh vigor and expectations, towards the distant, always calling, always receding, glaring and shining, sonorous and wonderful horizons!

There are many aspects of this natural transfiguration of our image of the world. But all this passes, as the world itself passes, and all this shining splendor dies away and is felt and recognized as delusion. The soul is longing for eternal satisfaction and rest, for something that remains, immutable and undying.

The world passes, life is swallowed, is subjugated by death. The soul yearns for such a transfiguration in which death is eliminated, in which the world becomes really and *substantially changed,* finally changed, and in which it is delivered from death and sin and evil and suffering, death being "swallowed up into victory" and eliminated.

4.

This is the Christian promise, the Christian hope: the *finality* of deliverance, the final and total triumph of Life Eternal; and this promise and hope is, as we have seen, the necessary consequence, the outcome of the fact *that has already taken place,* of a victory that has been won already. This is the peculiar feature of the Christian message: its thoroughgoing hope, its certainty of the coming, the final total Transfiguration.

We look, according to His promise, for a new heaven and a new earth, where dwelleth righteousness (II Peter 3:13). "God will be all in all (I Cor. 15:28). "And God shall wipe away all tears from their eyes; and there shall be no more death neither sorrow, nor crying, neither shall there be any more pain: for the former things are passed away. And He that sat on the throne said: Behold I make all things new . . ." "And there shall be no more curse, but the throne

of God and the Lamb shall be therein; and His servants shall
serve Him. And they shall see His face and His name shall
be on their foreheads. And there shall be no night any more,
and they need no light of a candle, neither light of the sun,
for God shall lighten upon them and they shall reign for
ever and ever" (Rev. 21: 4-8, 22: 3-5).

Without this certainty the Christian message is incom-
plete. There must be a total victory of the Lord, a total manifestation of His victory. Our present unsatisfactory, imperfect
reality, subject to evil and death and suffering, shall be lifted
up into the reality of Life Eternal. And evil there shall be
no more, neither death nor crying nor sorrow.

But *already* now, His Presence has illuminated our outlook and begins to transfigure our life. Already now there is
a change, if we want to accept it. "Behold, old things have
passed away, all things have become new," exclaims the
Apostle (II Cor. 5:17). We see it in the life of the saints.
Sometimes our own lives are touched and lit up by the rays
of this dawn. "God who said: From darkness the light shall
shine—has shone into our hearts to illuminate them to the
knowledge of His Glory in the face of Jesus Christ" (II Cor.
4:6). There are new elements of a new life entering our life
already now: the glory of Christ in which we participate
already now, if we are *co-crucified with Him*. That is the
mystery of the life of the saints: their clinging to Him, their
becoming one with Him, sharing His obedience and His
Cross. This is the *bliss* of the Cross and the life of the Spirit,
vouchedsafe already now to those who share with Christ His
obedience and His self-surrender.

The mystery of the life of the saints, of those who have
lived or even now live among us, is that a new reality begins
already to take shape in their persons. There is already a
beginning transformation of their persons "from glory to
glory." That such saints are, that such a transformation really
takes place, is one of the most palpable and eloquent tokens
of a higher transfigured reality, a reality already here and
dawning upon us. There are many narratives hinting at
this new plane—the plane of the life in the Spirit. In the

Sayings of the Fathers of the Egyptian desert we read, for example:

> Abbot Lot came once to see Abbot Joseph and said unto him: "Abbot, to the measure of my forces I try to fulfill my rule of life: I observe my little fast, I pray, I contemplate, I keep silence and I try to purify my thoughts. What ought I to do more?" The old man stood up and stretched his hands towards heaven. And his fingers became as ten burning candles. And he said then to Abbot Lot: "If you want, become wholly like fire."

Deeds of outgoing, self-forgetting love and the spirit of meekness, of boundless humility are also the marks of this new plane of life, of this beginning transfiguration. Isaac of Syria thus describes the signs announcing the nearness of this land of promise:

> This will be a sign to thee that thou art near the entrance of this land: when grace so begins to open thy eyes, that they begin to see the things essentially, then shall thy eyes pour forth tears that will stream, and the power of thy senses will be subdued so that henceforth they will be peacefully shut within thee. If anybody teaches thee differently, don't believe him . . . The heart becomes quite small and as soon as thou startest to pray tears are streaming—that is the sign that the cloud of grace has begun to repose upon the tabernacle of thy heart.

The greatest expression of this new reality of the Spirit is the power of burning, self-forgetting love—"There is no greater love than when one gives up his soul for his neighbors"—and boundless humility. The same Issac of Syria writes:

> When thou art lying before God in prayer, then be in thy consideration as an ant and as the reptiles of the earth and as a beetle. And stammer as a villager,

and speak not before Him with knowledge. With a
childlike mind approach unto God and walk before
Him, that thou mayest be worthy of the paternal cares
which fathers entertain on behalf of their little children.

This state of mind is the beginning of the Kingdom of
God on earth. Macarius of Egypt, referring to the vision of
the mysterious chariot in the Book of Ezechiel, describes how
elect souls become already on earth "living chariots moved by
the Spirit," how they become "all fire, all eye," glorious living
thrones of the King of Glory.

5.

For a changed, transfigured eye the whole of life begins
to be transfigured. Jacob Böhme speaks of the new vision
that presented itself to his spiritual eye: "The triumph that
was in my spirit, I cannot write or speak, nor can it be compared with anything save with the birth of life in the midst
of death, with the resurrection of the dead. In this light my
spirit straightway looked through all things and saw God
in all created things, even in the herbs and the grass."[3] So
also for the Persian mystic, the sufi and dervish Baba Kuhi
from Shiraz, the whole world is transfigured by his experience
of God: "I opened my eyes and through the radiance of His
countenance around me, in everything that my eyes perceived
I saw only God!"[4] Another sufi, Jelal eddin Rumi, is aware
how the whole world is flooded with waves of love. "Every
moment," he says, "from the right hand and from the left
soundeth the voice of love."[5] A great Indian mystic, Kabir,
cries: "Open the eyes of love and behold Him that pervadeth
the whole world! Consider it well, and know that this is your
own country!" "I see with eyes open and smile, and behold

[3]Jacob Böhme, "Aurora," XIX, 11-13.
[4]Quoted in Reynolds A. Nicholson, *The Mystics of Islam* (1914), p. 59.
[5]*Selected Poems from the "Divani Shamsi Tabriz,"* edited and translated
by Reynolds A. Nicholson (1898), No. IX, p. 33.

His beauty everywhere. I utter His name and whatever I see, it reminds me of Him; whatever I do, it becomes His worship . . ."[6]

Alas! this personal, emotional experience does not change the present state of the world. Evil can be denied by those Indian and Persian mystics, but it is not abolished. The real transfiguration is not an emotional or psychological one and not one that ignores evil and sin and the power of death. The real transfiguration is the one that uproots them, that overcomes and vanquishes them. The Christian believes that this has taken place through the Incarnation, the Death and the Resurrection of the Son of God. It is an incarnational outlook and an incarnational mysticism, and the transfiguration of the creature is the result of the Incarnation, because the Word has been made Flesh—and because He conquered death. We still continue to die, but "our life is concealed with Christ in God" and it shall be manifested in full at the end of time.

6.

In the sacrament of the eucharist we have an anticipation, a short glimpse of the future glory. The heavenly plane, the higher reality is brought near to us in this sacrament of the Lord's Supper. The center thereof is both the coming of the Glorified Lord to His faithful and the "proclaiming" of His death and His sacrifice. We live again His sacrifice that has been offered for us, once and for all times on earth, on the Mount of Golgotha, and that is being offered by Him eternally on the heavenly altar in continuous intercession for us before the Father.

And I saw in the midst of the throne and of the four living creatures, and in the midst of the elders a Lamb standing, as though it had been slain . . . And I saw, and I heard a voice of many angels round about the throne and the living creatures and the elders; and

[6]*One Hundred Poems of Kabir* . . . LXXVI, XLI.

the number of them was ten thousand times ten thousand, and thousands of thousands; saying with a great
voice: Worthy is the Lamb that hath been slain to
receive the power, and riches, and wisdom, and might,
and honour, and glory, and blessing. (Rev. 5:6a,
11-12).

That is the eternal prototype of the liturgy. The liturgy
is a piece of heavenly experience, of the heavenly reality
present here among us. At the same time it is rooted in history,
it is historical reality—and glory, a contemplation of transfigured history and of the eternal household-plan of God.

The Church is uplifted to these heights—to the contemplation of the eternal sacrifice of the Lamb and at the same
time of His historical death and historical self-dedication for
us. Here history and eternity blend together. And so the Lord
that comes to His faithful is the Lord who comes willingly
to be sacrificed. Compare for example this song of the Eastern
Church:

> Let all mortal flesh be silent and stand with fear and
> trembling . . . For the King of Kings and the Lord of
> Lords comes to be sacrificed and to give Himself as
> food to the faithful . . .

And at the same time—as we saw—He is the Glorified Lord,
the Risen One, the Victor and King of Kings, surrounded by
hosts of angels, "born on a shield invisibly by hosts of angels."
"Lo, the King of Glory enters. Lo, the mystical sacrifice is
fulfilled and ushered in."

The heavenly world is taking part in the liturgy. But more
than that: the mysterious Host, the Crucified One and the
Living One, is entering the souls and the bodies of the faithful
and hallows them, preparing them for Life Eternal. He comes
to the individual soul that bows before Him in deepest self-
condemnation and repentance, feeling herself unworthy that
He should enter under the roof of her house: "for it is all
empty and crumbling to pieces." But He enters and heals and
sanctifies soul and body. And He comes also to the whole of

the Church, and our common partaking of the One Bread
makes us all *one* Body. But the eucharist points also to the
sanctification and transfiguration of the whole created world.
The wine from the grapes and the vineyards and the bread
from the wheat of the field become His transfigured, His
glorified Blood and Body.[7] They are promises of the nature
which will be sanctified and glorified because the Word
has become Flesh and has suffered and has conquered death.
So the eucharist points also to the future plenitude, to His
future coming in glory. "You proclaim the death of the Lord,
till He comes" (I Cor. 11:26). The past—His historical death
on Golgotha and His Resurrection—is mysteriously united to
His unutterable Presence—the Presence of the Glorified One,
who is the One who presents Himself in sacrifice, and the
Risen One simultaneously. And this mysterious flowing
together of historical fact and mystical Presence is also a
stretching forward to the fulness of the manifestation of His
glory.

Not the eucharistic sacrifice alone, but the whole Church
is a living sacrament in which history and Divine Presence,
concrete historical fact—as basis and *contents* of the Good
Tidings—and the Divine Life, the life of the Spirit that is
permeating the whole Body, are united in *one* stream. And
this stream stretches forward—to the future fulness of revelation. The Church fights her way. She must be cleansed, she
must grow—"to the full measure of the stature of Christ." In
her the bodily, the earthly, the creaturely must be sanctified
by the force of the Spirit.

7.

There is a peculiar kind of transfiguration, of immense
importance, closely connected with our life as members of
the Church of God: the new approach to the fellow-man, the
new conception and experience of the fellow-man—in Christ.
Our brother has changed, has immensely increased in his
hidden value for the enlightened eye. "Don't despise one of

---

[7]See Irenaeus, *Adv. Haereses* V, 2, 2-3.

these little ones: for I tell you their angels in heaven always see the face of the Heavenly Father." What we have done to one of those least ones, we have done to Christ, the eldest Brother. For He is mystically present in all those least ones. That makes the value of the brother immense. When we feed the hungry, when we give drink to the thirsty, or clothe the naked, or receive in our homes the homeless, or visit the sick and the prisoner, we open sudden vistas, or rather sudden vistas can be opened on us, vistas that are anticipations of the coming realm of Life Eternal. It is a mystical encounter with the Lord in the person of the suffering brother. A life dedicated to the suffering brother is a life on which dawns the Eternal Reality—the reality of the immense, outgoing, self-giving love of God, which is at the root of all existence, of all reality. To live in it *is Life Eternal.* And already here glimpses of this Life Eternal, of the future transfiguration can be given to us, transfiguring us by the power of love—His love—which streaming through us, transfigures in our eyes the brethren and even more—this can help them also to be uplifted unto this new life of *transfiguration by love,* of being conquered by love, of being redeemed by love.

This is the sense of Christ's sacrifice, the sense of His coming to earth, the sense of the Good Tidings. But it is made clear to us *not so much through books as through participation in His service of love, in His sacrifice of love.* As Paul wrote to the Corinthians: "Now I rejoice in my sufferings for your sake and I make up what is lacking of the sufferings of Christ in my flesh on behalf of His Body which is the Church" (I Cor. 1:24). This is the ultimate sense of the Church of God: to be jointly, all of us together, taken hold of by this power of love. And this is the real beginning of transfiguration, the first glimpse of the eternal Kingdom of God—here on our earth, amidst all its sufferings and in-justices.

And therefore already now in Him *peace is given to us.* The whole story of humanity is a struggle for peace, for real peace of the heart. "Fecisti nos Domine, ad te, et inquietum est cor nostrum, donec requiescat in te," wrote Augustine ("You made us for Yourself, O Lord, and our heart is restless until it rests in You"). "My peace I leave you, My peace I give unto you," are the words of comfort that Christ addressed to His disciples during the last discourse before His passion.

A whole program, a promise and more than that: a reality, is given in these words—the reality of a life which begins to be transfigured in strife and struggle, in manliness and meekness, in humility and suffering and death, but also in the power of God, with a trustful, child-like self-surrender unto His will, which means peace to us. "La Sua volunta è nostra pace," says Dante. And tasting already now of this peace, given to us as to little children, we know that it will grow to the boundless peace of God that transcends all knowledge. But the process of transfiguration has to start and has started already—here and now.

10

The Atonement

1.

The mystery of the atonement is a continuous, lasting mystery. The atonement lasts till now, it is permanent. It is historical and eternal. It has taken place once—at the central point of history—and it works continuously in the eternal self-offering of the Lamb standing before the throne of the Father, "as if it were slain" in permanent intercession, as the seer has seen in the Revelation (chapter 5). Pascal felt deeply this mystical reality when he said that Christ suffers continuously for us; we should not sleep whilst He is suffering. And Origen, commenting the words of the Baptist: "Look, there is the Lamb of God that takes away the sins of the world," points to the fact that these words refer not only to a past happening, but also to the incessant act of a permanent taking away of sins: "Continuously does He achieve the taking away of the sins from every individual man that is in the world, until the sin is taken away from the whole world" (Commentary on John 1:37). There is a *continuous mystery of redemption* working in the world. It has taken place once historically —once for all, not to be repeated in history—and it continues to work eternally: in the mystery of His permanent self-offering to the Father in intercession for us and in the mystery of our co-crucifixion with Him. The self-sacrifice, the self-surrender of the Son of God, being one and indivisible, presents accordingly two aspects: the historical fact, unique and decisive once for ever: "It is consummated!" (the last words of the Crucified, according to the Fourth Gospel); and the mystical continuous standing of the crucified and glorified Lord before the throne of the Father in unceasing intercession.

2.

What is the sense of the atonement? It is the revelation of boundless, conquering Divine Love, of boundless, most radical, most humble—so boundless that it cannot be sufficiently realized, imagined and thought out—Divine Condescension. That is the essence of the atonement. "God so loved the world, that He gave His only-begotten Son" (John 3:16). "In this the love of God manifested itself, that God sent into the world His only-begotten Son in order that we might get life through Him." "In this have we known love, that He has laid down His life for us" (I John 4: 3-16). The whole mystery of salvation is in this boundless manifestation of love, this boundless and conquering humility and self-surrender. There are two sides to this one stream of redemption that has entered the world: the one is flowing manward, coming from God, and this is decisive; the other is directed Godwards, coming from man, but this flowing Godwards is also the work of God, being the obedient self-surrender of the Son of God, our Brother by blood and flesh, and the real representative of mankind. And both sides of the process are one stream.

The meaning and basis of the atonement is the love of God. Only this is the inspiring and conquering force thereof, not any idea of juridicial justification, of forensic litigation. All is taking place on a far deeper, far more substantial level —on the divine level, on the level of what God really is, essentially is, revealed in the boundless love of God and in the self-surrender of His Son.

This reality of the infinite loving condescension of God, creative and conquering, has been the basis and keystone, yea, the essence, the only and supreme contents of the whole Christian message, for all times and generations. The Eastern Church sings in her hymns, overwhelmed by deepest admiration and wonder: "Thou, O Life, hast been put in the grave, O Christ, and the host of angels shuddered seeing Thy condescension." "Thou camest upon earth in order to save Adam, and not having found him there, Thou descendest even to hell in search of him." There is no measure and no reckoning in this condescension; it surpasses all computation. This is emphasized *e.g.* in the mystical experience of the English mystic Lady Julian of Norwich (14th century): "If I could have suffered more, says Christ, I would have suffered more. But there could not be greater suffering!" And this makes *e.g.* Francis of Assisi and the Fathers of the East speak of the boundlessness and inscrutable depth of the loving and humble condescension of God. "O humilitas sublimis! O sublimitas humilis!" exclaims Francis like Julian of Norwich; and seven centuries earlier, Isaac of Syria (7th century) says in his Homilies: "God has delivered His Son to die on the Cross, because of His Love for the creature. If He had something more precious, He would have given it also in order to acquire mankind." The boundlessness of His condescension is stressed by Irenaeus of Lyon: "He has kindly poured Himself out, in order to gather us into the nest of the Father."[1]

The summit of "His pouring Himself out," of His self-surrender is His agony in Gethsemane and on the Cross, and His words on the Cross and His death. "When He was left alone by His Father on the cross," says Gregory of Nyssa, "He represented then our situation. He is called and is really man in order to sanctify men by His person, having become as it were a leaven for the whole lump." Origen (Commentary on Psalm 21) dwells on the words: "My God, my God, why hast Thou forsaken me?" "They point to the depth of His condescension; these words of Our Lord represent our suffering. We were left alone and rejected, but now we are again accepted and are saved by the suffering of Him who is beyond suffering, when He took upon Himself our sickness and our sin." And Gregory of Nazianzen writes: "He complained together with us on the Cross that God had forsaken Him" (Homily on the Incarnation).

The Church in east, west, north and south has contem-

[1] *Adv. Haereses* V, 2, 1.

plated and adored this mystery of the outpouring of Divine
Love, boundless and measureless, as already it had been contemplated by John the Divine: "In this the love of God
towards us revealed itself, that God sent into the world His
only-begotten Son in order that we might receive life through
Him. Therein is love, not that we love God, but that He
loved us and sent His Son to be the propitiation for our sins"
(I John 4: 9-10). And Christ Himself, according to the
Fourth Gospel, had emphasized it in the parable of the Good
Shepherd: "I am the Good Shepherd; the Good Shepherd
lays down his soul for his sheep . . . I am the Good Shepherd,
and I know those that are mine, and those that are mine know
me . . . I lay down my life for the sheep. Therefore does the
Father love me that I surrender it. I have the power to surrender it, and the power to take it again. This commandment
I received from my Father."

The abyss is filled up through the initiative of God. Not
we loved Him, but He loved us first. And bearers of this
message, the witnesses of this fact, are as it were "ambassa-
dors" for Christ: "as though God did beseech you through us,
we pray you in Christ's stead 'be you reconciled to God' "
(II Cor. 5: 20). God reconciles us to Himself by the act of
supreme self-surrender. He so to say tries to win us by His
love. There is the infinite dynamic activity of God filling up
the chasm and winning us and inviting us to be reconciled
with Him. For we have to be won, and we must be reconciled
with God in the most central and intimate recesses of our
personality; and that leads us to the other side of the act of
atonement: pointing Godwards from man.

3.

We must be won, we have to be reconciled with God. The
chasm has to be filled up not only from the divine side, through
His measureless condenscension: we must be taken hold of by
the force of this condenscension, and turn to God and surrender ourselves to Him and submit ourselves to Him in
perfect obedience. That is the other side of the fact and pro-

cess of redemption: not only the Son of God "poured Himself out" in infinite, condenscending and conquering love, but we also have to submit to God, to make our will submit to His in free and loving obedience. Can we do that? Can we attain this goal? The religious history of mankind on its summits is an attempt of heroically-minded men to surrender themselves to the will of God. We find this desire stated *e.g.* in many Indian and Islamic mystical texts, as in the *Bhagavat Gita,* in the words of Krishna to Arjuna: "All that thou doest, that thou eatest, that thou offerest in sacrifice, that thou layest upon thyself as an ascetic exercise—all that, O son of Kunti, make as a gift to Me." "Among all the yogis the man who surrenders to Me his innermost self and with faith adores Me, is the nearest to Me." And the modern Indian mystic Tagore writes in one of his poems: "Let only the smallest thing remain from me, that I might say: Thou are all." And we have wonderful examples of such obedient self-surrender to God among Islamic saints and mystics as well.

But from the Christian point of view there rises an objection: no such total surrender is possible to man. It is only an idea, a glimpse, a nostalgia that haunts the thoughts and feelings of those mystics, those leading representatives of mankind in its aspirations and its travelling and yearning and tending Godwards. There is always a remainder of selfishness, of self-concentration, self-admiration sticking to man's heart, even in his utter self-emptying, self-surrender. There remains always the feeling: "I have surrendered my will to God." And so no real self-surrender or total obedience has really taken place through all those endeavors, although this free obedience, this free surrender of one's will to God is the *pivot* of the world's religious and moral history. But it could not be achieved. It was self-delusion when men thought they had or they could achieve that. The Christian believes that it has been achieved once: in the total obedience of the Son of God who "has become obedient unto death, even the death of the cross" (Philip. 2:8). Being really fully man in the full possession of all the distinctive features of humanity, except sin, he could represent mankind in its way Godwards.

4.

The atonement works in us. What has been achieved by Christ is not only a representative act, a mystical symbol. It is much more than that: it transforms in a most essential and basic way our internal life, our relation with God, yes, all our situation in the world, the destiny of all our personality, soul and body, and the destiny of the whole cosmos. But let us return to our spiritual life. *We have to become obedient in Christ.* That is the sense of the atonement for us. He has become obedient to the Father as true representative of the human race, as true "High Priest" (according to the image much used by the church Fathers, *e.g.* by Gregory of Nyssa). But—and not symbolically only—in Him we also become obedient: by sharing His Cross. Only so can the redemption, wrought by the Son of God who was also really Son of Man, work in us. That makes the Cross to be the pivot of all our interior life, the presupposition and also the way of our salvation. If we don't share His Cross, we are not partakers of His Life Eternal. We have received *gratis,* without any merit on our side, as the great gift, the great boon, to share His obedience, to become obedient through Him and in Him. This is not passive or mechanical. We are led by obedience to become ourselves actively and consciously obedient to the Heavenly Father, to become active and conscious sharers of His Son's Cross. This makes the doctrine of co-crucifixion with Christ central in the teaching of Paul, central in the Christian life and Christian outlook. And here we approach also the mystery of suffering, of the redeeming quality of suffering. Not our suffering is redeeming: His suffering is redeeming as of the unblemished, immaculate, the voluntary self-delivering Victim; but our suffering receives—we shall return to this subject—a redeeming quality if merged in His suffering, if uplifted by His suffering (Col. 1:24), if having become a *part* of His *eternal sacrifice,* offering His will in obedience to His father on the "glorious" and "life-giving" Cross, reconciling the heavenly and the earthly.

5.

"It pleased the Father," writes Paul to the Colossians, "that in Him should dwell all the plenitude; and through Him to reconcile all things to Himself; through Him, I say, whether they be things of earth or things in heaven" (Col. 1: 19-21). Here, as in other analogous utterings of Paul, vistas are opening into the *cosmical* significance of the atonement, surpassing by far its purely human implications. In the atonement is given the beginning of the return of the whole fallen creature, fallen through the disobedience of man to God. The act of the return has been started by the perfect obedience of the "Second Adam," the new Head of the redeemed humanity, the Son of God who became Son of Man. The victory has already been won and sealed by the blood of the Lamb of God. Now it has to become manifested; it has to be realized more and more, until it permeates the whole bulk of creation.

11

The Humility of God

1.

The idea of the humility of God seems strange. It is nevertheless true. It is one of the greatest truths that dawn upon us when we consider the universe and man in their history; I mean, when we consider them from a Christian viewpoint. Then this truth reveals itself in its unutterable grandeur. More than that: it can take hold of us with sudden overwhelming poignancy, in which the sense of trembling reverence and wonder and loving adoration are blended into one.

The humility of God discloses itself already in the act of creation. He has willed that there should be life "and life in abundance." It did not diminish His glory and splendor, it enhanced His glory and splendor; but He wanted that some things should exist "outside" of Him, as something separated from Him and yet deeply united with Him, as something "independent," although at the same time it was and remained in deepest dependence on Him. He voluntarily restricted His might and His power in admitting a thing beside Him, utterly dependent on Him but still having its own individuality, its own physiognomy, received from God but still *its own.*

That is creation. The creation does not limit the omnipotence of the Creator—on the contrary, it is the most eloquent proof thereof—, but it makes that something which exists beside God, which is not God. And therein the greatness and glory of God reveal themselves with special splendor, but

also the humility of God. For this is self-restriction, loving
self-restriction. It is love. For love is humble and creative and
restricts itself, "forgets" itself and promotes the welfare of
the beloved. The Son of Man, who was Son of God, said of
Himself: "I came in order that they should have life and
have it in abundance." The same words could be inscribed
over the whole act of creation. The idea of the self-com-
municating, outflowing love—creative and resplendent in its
outgoing "humility" and in its majesty and power (the "humility" being one of the most characteristic and fundamental
aspects of its majesty and glory and power)—this idea of the
outgoing, out-flowing creative love is admirably expressed by
Dante in his "Paradiso":

> Non per aver à se di bon aquisto
> Ch'esser non può, ma perchè il suo splendore
> Potesse risplendendo, dir: subsisto,
> —In sua Eternità, di tempo fuore
> Fuor d'ogni altro comprender, come i piacque,
> S'aperse in nuovi amori l'Eterno Amore.

("Not in order to gain any benefit for Himself, which would
be impossible, but so that His splendor, shining back, might
say: 'I am,'—in His Eternity, beyond time, beyond every other
limit, as it pleased Him, the Eternal Love revealed Himself
in new loves."—XXIX, 13-18)

The Eternal Love willed that other individual love-centers
should exist beside it and share its bliss. That according to
Dante is the meaning of creation.

This is the "humility" of God, but this humility is also
the enhanced manifestation of His glory. For the glory of
God is resplendent in His works and in His creation.

2.

The guidance of humanity through the different stages of
its history is also an act of the condescension of God, of

God's loving humility. He has not left quite alone, has not quite forsaken those poor blundering men, those tribes and nations and races. So often has His image been misrepresented and distorted, but still He has been continually looked for and searched for and sometimes there came a distant hint, a dark inkling of His real being, for again and again He was vouchsafing some glimpses of Himself to searching hearts amidst the dark clouds of human ignorance and superstitions, human passions, and human corruption and bestiality. Sometimes He has been even dimly felt and hinted at as the Condescending One. So in old China we have the marvelous mystical intuition of Lao-Tse about the boundless humility of the Absolute Principle of all life and being—the Supreme Tao ("The Way"):

> Tao is all-pervading, and its age is inexhaustible!
> Fathomless! It is like the fountain-head of all things . . .
> From Him all things take their rise, but He does not
>   turn away from them;
> He gives them life, but does not take possession of
>   them;
> He acts, but does not appropriate;
> Accomplishes, but claims no credit . . .

And again:

> The Great Tao flows everywhere . . .
> The myriad things derive their life from it,
> And it does not deny them . . .
> It clothes and feeds the myriad things,
> Yet does not claim them as its own . . .
> Being the home of all things, yet claiming not,
> It must be considered great:
> Because to the end it does not claim greatness,
> Its greatness is achieved . . .

And therefore the author exclaims again and again in marvel and amazement: "O how marvellous and silent! O how unfathomable!"

This is a deep and beautiful glimpse of the Divine Reality,
but it remains a general statement, vague, impersonal and
abstract. It lacks the poignancy of a definite personality, of an
historical fact. For amidst the brittle frame of history, in a
concrete fact of historical human existence, decisions of universal, yea cosmic scope, have taken place, solutions of a final,
of a decisive, victorious and triumphant character, decisions
that were at the same time historical *events*. There is therefore a character of poignancy, of uniqueness, of moral direct-
ness in this Christian message that addresses you in a personal
way, that appeals to you as to a living individual person,
because a concrete living Person, our Brother according to
flesh and blood and our sharer in moral struggle and effort
and moral heroism, is the bearer of this message, of this
Truth—the condescension of God—or rather is the embodiment of this condescension: the Divine Word that became
man, God that has become our Brother. The humility is thus
far more striking and much more far-reaching and radical,
because it is the expression not of a pantheistic creed in which
God and the whole of the universe essentially coincide, but
the manifestation of a living personal God, holy and unattainable to creature, Creator and Master of all things that willingly, out of His own loving initiative became creature, in
order to come near to us and to have us as His own, as His
friends and brothers, and take hold of us and move our
hearts, and to transfigure us and to redeem us. Thus the
"humility" of God is only another term for something greater
than all things—the condescending love of God.

3.

The Christ of the Gospels is humble. That is the mark
under which He enters history. It is the all-pervading mark.
In the chapter 12 of the Gospel according to Matthew the
words of Isaiah are referred to Him, thus characterizing His
personality: "Behold My Servant whom I have chosen, My
Beloved, in whom My soul is well pleased . . . He shall not
strive, nor cry; neither shall any man hear His voice in the

streets. A bruised reed shall He not break, and a smoking flax shall He not quench . . ."

The manger, the homeless life of travel, teaching and service, interwoven with persecutions which He underwent from the hand of His enemies, His arrest, trial, passion, crucifixion and death—all this is, as is well known, *one* great revelation of deepest humility and self-sacrificing love. But mark how this humility, this meekness ("Learn from Me, for I am meek and humble of heart") is at the same time permeated by the touch of majesty. A supreme Presence is given in this meekness and humility.

It is a royal humility, the meekness of majesty; it is the humility of God. How this all-permeating touch of a supreme Presence runs *e.g.* through all these words: "Come unto Me you that labor and are heavy-laden, and I will give you rest. Take My yoke upon you and learn from Me: for I am meek and humble in heart, and you shall find rest unto your souls." The redeeming, peace-giving, restoring and healing Presence, this Center and Fulfillment, the Presence of One Who is greater than Sabbath, greater than Solomon, before Whom the man born blind, now healed, falls down and "worships Him," Whose coming into the house of Zacchaeus is a decisive turning point in the life of this sinful man, Whose word moves and strikes hearts and sets them afire, Who has the power to pardon sins but also to heal and to raise from the bed of sickness—this Presence that is felt by John the Baptist as of One before Whom he has totally to eclipse himself, not worthy even "to stoop down and to unloose the latches of His shoes"—this Presence, I say, is not only clad and hidden in humility, but His humility is the most appropriate, the most adequate *revelation* of the greatness of this Presence, the unutterable, boundless greatness of God being revealed in his unutterable, boundless humility. That is the center of Paul's preaching: "He has humbled Himself becoming obedient unto death" (Phil. 2).

This is the vision that made Francis of Assisi, who contemplated it incessantly with the eye of burning love, to exclaim (referring to the eucharist): "O sublimitas humilis! O humilitas sublimis!" This is the vision from which the

Eastern Orthodox Church cannot detach its gaze in trembling thankfulness, love and awe-stricken admiration. The two *poles* are contemplated simultaneously, as they both are simultaneously given in the Incarnate Son of God—the suffering humanity and the fulness of God.

In an indescribable manner God unites Himself with man . . . the earthly reaches to heaven, the world is freed from the ancient curse, creation exults with joy (*Annunciation hymn*).

Today heaven and earth are made one in the Birth of Christ. Today God has descended upon the earth, and man has ascended to the heaven (*Christmas hymn*).

Thou hast become poor like us, and hast deified the earthly by Thy union with it. (*Christmas hymn*).

And these are the contemplative hymns of Holy Week:

Today He who hung the earth upon the waters is hung on the tree. The King of the Angels is decked with a crown of thorns. He who wraps the heavens in clouds is wrapped in the purple of mockery. He who freed Adam in the Jordan is slapped on the face. The Bridegroom of the Church is affixed to the cross with nails. The Son of the Virgin is pierced by a spear. We worship Thy passion, O Christ. We worship Thy passion, Christ. We worship Thy passion, O Christ. Show us also Thy glorious resurrection!

Today the Master of Creation stands before Pilate. The Creator is given over to die on a cross. As a lamb He is voluntarily led to slaughter. He is nailed, His side is pierced, His lips are moistened with gall. The Redeemer of all is struck on the cheek. The Creator of all is mocked by His own creatures. What a great love the Master shows for men. He prayed to His Father even for those who put Him to death: Father, forgive them, for they know not what they do.

O Life, how canst Thou die? How canst Thou dwell in the grave? But Thou destroyest the dominion of death and raisest the dead from the depths of hell.

We glorify Thee, O King Jesus, and we worship Thy burial and Thy passion, whereby Thou hast redeemed us from corruption.

Thou that didst set the measure of the earth today dwellest in a narrow grave, O Jesus, King of all, that raisest the dead from the graves.

O Jesus, my Christ, Lord of all, why didst Thou descend to those who are in hell? Was it for the redemption of mankind?

The master of the universe is seen as dead, and He that has emptied the graves of their dead is laid in a new tomb.

O Christ the Life, Thou hast descended into the grave, and through Thy death Thou hast destroyed death, and life hast Thou made to stream forth for all the world.

Majesty in humility! Life Eternal in death and overcoming death! A great Orthodox teacher of spiritual life, Philotheus of Sinai, writes accordingly: "All the saints clothed themselves with this supreme holy garment of God": humility.[1]

We are in a world that bewilders us, that always has bewildered man. We feel ourselves helpless, lost in the world's immensity, crushed by the natural course of happenings, baffled and disappointed. How are we to account for all the tragic side of man's life encountering us, so to say, at every step, lurking from every corner, from every issue of the usual morning paper, with its catastrophes, burning airplanes, railroad accidents, explosions in mines, innundations, war casualties? And what of our personal life drifting imperceptibly into the great chasm that is the end and limit of

[1] *Dobrotolubiye* (*Philokalia*), 2nd Russian ed. (1900), vol. II, p. 406.

our life here? And what of this perpetual flow of changes, the ever-flowing, incessant, untiring stream of decay, of mutability, of passing away? And of the silence of the immense expanses giving no answer, void of response to our anguish, to our appeal, to our challenge, and seeming to be void of a higher Presence? "Le silence de ces espaces infinis m'effraie," said Pascal. What is the meaning of this silent, crushing, implacable and unresponsive universe, of its life and decay and passing away, crumbling to pieces and rebirth in the millions and billions of astronomical years? What is the bearing, the intimate hidden sense of this universe, its life, its laws, its structure, its silence, its cold magnificence, and the step of death marching through it? What is the sense of our passing joys and sorrows, lives and deaths? Is there not in this whirlwind of deaths and lives, soon to be forgotten, to leave no trace behind them, a strain of the deep vanity of all things, a taste of unredeemed, unutterable bitterness and disappointment? Nothing could be said against this presentation of the world's life and personal existence and the utter senselessness of the awfulness of every life and every existence, if there had not been a decisive and exhaustive revelation of the world's "background," of the secret sources of Eternal Life, eternal production, eternal reality behind the structure of this world. This revelation of the secret "springs" of all life, all reality—and also of the *sense of life,* for life has got a sense—was the active, condescending self-disclosure of the love of God. God revealed Himself in "the Son of His love." There is no void—all is full of His nearness. Even in sufferings, in death, in utter dereliction He is near. He is there—having descended Himself into the abyss of suffering and death and love. His love having brought Him to do so. "This is love, not that we loved God but that He loved us and sent His Son as the expiation for our sins" (I John 4:10).

There is a sense, an aim, a plan in the mystery of the world. The revelation of God in His Incarnate Son, as condescending, creating and restoring love, is the nerve of the world's life, the hidden mystery of all being and becoming, transfiguring life even in the deepest abysses of our and the world's existence.

12

The Law of Love

1.

The supreme law is the law of love. Even God was subjugated by the power of love, even God could not escape
the power of love, say Christian mystical writers and saints
of different countries and centuries. But this language, im-
pressive and beautiful though it be, is not quite adequate.
The power of love is God's being itself; it is the innermost
mystery, the innermost nerve, the spring and the goal of the
life of the world. It is not a sudden rush, a sudden movement:
it is the innermost law and foundation of existence, as far
as it is in God. But we and the world can fall outside of
God, and this did happen and our vision became thus obscured, and other spiritual forces began to rule over us and
over the fallen world, forces of destruction, of hatred, of
blind, egotistical self-affirmation, which means degradation,
of injustice, of untruth, of suffering, of instability, of death.
Our life is subjected to them; so is the life of our world. But
these are not the ultimate depths of life: in its ultimate
depths the creation listens to the Word of God and yearns
for redemption and knocks at the doors of mercy. In these
depths of life there is a dialogue between the life-giving
and redeeming God and creation. And history is the fulfillment of the plan of the merciful God, His plan of redemption, of salvation, of reintegration of all things, His "household-plan," the vision of which has so deeply impressed and
conquered the mind of Paul. So the moving spring of history,

in spite of all its troubles and catastrophes, is the guiding
and reintegrating and educating and redeeming love of God.

The medieval seer, Lady Julian of Norwich, thus formu-
lates the meaning of all she had seen, of all that had been
revealed to her, the sense of the world's being and history: "Wouldst thou learn thy Lord's meaning in this thing?
Learn it well: Love was His meaning.—Who showed it thee?
—Love.—What showed He thee?—Love.—Wherefore showed
it He?—For Love."

2.

Let us throw a short and reverential glance, a glance full
of deepest humility and trembling adoration, at the mystery
of God Himself, God as the outflowing power of love, who
is love Himself in His innermost life, independently of the
world and its being. In the "High-Priestly prayer" of Christ
we have glimpses of this reality. The depths of the relations
between Father and Son, and Son and Father, is love: "That
they all be one; as Thou, Father, art in Me, and I am in Thee,
so let them be one in Us . . ." "I in Thee, and Thou in
Me, that they may be made perfect in one, and that the
world may know that Thou hast sent Me and hast loved them,
as Thou hast loved Me." "Father, I will that they also, whom
Thou hast given Me, be with Me where I am; that they may
behold My glory which Thou hast given Me: for Thou
lovedst Me before the foundation of the world . . ." "And
I have declared unto them Thy name . . . that the love where-
with Thou hast loved Me, be in them, and I in them." (John
17: 21, 23, 24, 26).

"For Thou lovedst Me before the foundation of the world"
—a permanent revelation of love, He has given us glory and
grace "in the Beloved One"; He has led us into the Kingdom
of the Son of His love," says Paul (Eph. 1:6; Col. 1:13).
The Kingdom of the Son of His love, the love before the
foundation of the world—all that points to a relation beyond
and before all our possible experience: to the depths of Divine
Life. In these depths of His eternal life God is loving, before

the foundation of the world; and the eternal object of His love is the "Son of His love." This comes before all. That is why John can say: "God is Love"—Love by Himself, in Himself, not only in relation to us. And that is the religious, the essential significance of our faith in the Blessed Trinity: God is a Living God, a God that loves; *His own internal life is Love*. And the Spirit of God is the Spirit of Love.

This Love has revealed itself, and this Love wants us to love Him back, and this Love will vanquish. So the beginning is Love and the end is Love. And in the center stands His self-revelation in love and humility: the Cross of the Son of God. And our new life is love, only love, the all-transcending power of love. The goal of this new life is "to know the love of Christ that passes all knowledge," to be carried away by the love of Christ ("the love of Christ takes hold of us"), to vanquish all obstacles, even tortures and death, in this love of Christ: "we are more than conquerors through Him that loved us," for nothing, "neither death, nor life . . . nor things present, nor things to come, nor height, nor depth, nor any other creature shall be able to separate us from the love of God in Christ Jesus our Lord."

Here is a new rhythm of life, a new law of life—this love that "covers all, believes all, hopes all, endures all," that makes it possible to forgive the enemy, to pray for the enemy, that stretches itself forward in kindness, condescension and pardon towards one's enemy. Impossible to put down in strict rules, this is a new conquering force, a new life, a new law of life, a new inspiration. "Hereby we perceive love, that He laid down His life for us; and we ought to lay down our lives for the brethren" (I John 3: 16).

Augustine was right when instead of formulating external rules of moral conduct he made this bold enunciation: "Dilige et fac quod vis" ("Love, and do what you like"). He was really stating hereby the inner sense of the whole moral teaching of the Gospel.

But it is more than a moral teaching; it is a new force—the stream of divine love connecting heaven and earth and giving a sense, a direction to our lives still here on earth. This love is also a faith and a certainty. "And we have known the

love that God has to us and believed in it. God is love, and
who dwelleth in love, he dwelleth in God, and God in him"
(I John 4: 16). That is the law of the new life, beginning
already now, based on the revelation of His condescending
love and stretching forward. More than that: it is the supreme
law of Life Eternal.